LUDWIG
VAN
BEETHOVEN

GREAT ACHIEVERS
LIVES OF THE PHYSICALLY CHALLENGED

LUDWIG VAN BEETHOVEN

COMPOSER

Dynise Balcavage

Chelsea House Publishers

Philadelphia

COVER: Portrait of Beethoven by Joseph Karl Stieler, 1819. Photograph by Erich Lessing/Art Resource.

FRONTIS: Beethoven at the piano. Painting by M. Rodig.

CHELSEA HOUSE PUBLISHERS

EDITORIAL DIRECTOR Richard Rennert
ART DIRECTOR Sara Davis
PRODUCTION MANAGER Pamela Loos
PICTURE EDITOR Judy Hasday

Staff for **LUDWIG VAN BEETHOVEN**
SENIOR EDITOR John Ziff
EDITORIAL ASSISTANT Kristine Brennan
DESIGNER Takeshi Takahashi
PICTURE RESEARCHER Patricia Burns

First Printing

1 3 5 7 9 8 6 4 2

Library of Congress Cataloging-in-Publication Data

Balcavage, Dynise.
Ludwig van Beethoven, composer / Dynise Balcavage.
  p. cm. — (Great achievers: lives of the physically challenged)
Includes bibliographical references (p.) and index.
Summary: Narrates the life of the German-born musical genius who lost his hearing completely by age fifty and who is renowned as one of the world's greatest composers.

ISBN 0-7910-2082-7 (hc)

1. Beethoven, Ludwig van, 1770-1827—Juvenile literature. 2. Composers—Austria—Biography—Juvenile literature. [1. Beethoven, Ludwig van, 1770-1827. 2. Composers.] I. Series: Great achievers (Chelsea House Publishers)
ML3930.B4B35 1996
780.92—dc20   95-46395
 [B]   CIP
                                                   AC MN

CONTENTS

GREAT ACHIEVERS

LIVES OF THE PHYSICALLY CHALLENGED

A Message for Everyone

Jerry Lewis

Close to half a century ago—when I was the ripe old age of 23—an incredible stroke of fate rocketed me to overnight stardom as an entertainer. After the initial shock wore off, I began to have a very strong feeling that, in return for all life had given me, I must find a way of giving something back. At just that moment, a deeply moving experience in my personal life persuaded me to take up the leadership of a fledgling battle to defeat a then little-known group of diseases called muscular dystrophy, as well as other related neuromuscular diseases—all of which are disabling, and, in the worst cases, cut life short.

In 1950, when the Muscular Dystrophy Association (MDA)—of which I am national chairman—was established, physical disability was looked on as a matter of shame. Franklin Roosevelt, who guided America through World War II from a wheelchair, and Harold Russell, the World War II hero who lost both hands in battle, then became an Academy Award–winning movie star and chairman of the President's Committee on Employment of the Handicapped, were the exceptions. One of the reasons that muscular dystrophy and related diseases were so little known was that people who had been disabled by them were hidden at home, away from the pity and discomfort with which they were generally regarded by society. As I got to know and began working with people who have disabilities, I quickly learned what a tragic mistake this perception was. And my determination to correct this terrible problem soon became as great as my commitment to see disabling neuromuscular diseases wiped from the face of the earth.

I have long wondered why it never occurs to us, as we experience the knee-jerk inclination to feel sorry for people who are physically disabled, that lives such as those led by President Roosevelt, Harold Russell, and all of the extraordinary people profiled in this Great Achievers series demonstrate unmistakably how wrong we are. Physical disability need not be something that blights life and destroys opportunity for personal fulfillment and accomplishment. On the contrary, as people such as Ray Charles, Stephen Hawking, and Ron Kovic prove, physical disability can be a spur to greatness rather than a condemnation to emptiness.

In fact, if my experience with physically disabled people can be taken as a guide, as far as accomplishment is concerned, they have a slight edge on the rest of us. The unusual challenges they face require finding greater-than-average sources of energy and determination to achieve much of what able-bodied people take for granted. Often, this ultimately translates into a lifetime of superior performance in whatever endeavor people with disabilities choose to pursue.

If you have watched my Labor Day Telethon over the years, you know exactly what I am talking about. Annually, we introduce to tens of millions of Americans people whose accomplishments would distinguish them regardless of their physical conditions—top-ranking executives, physicians, scientists, lawyers, musicians, and artists. The message I hope the audience receives is not that these extraordinary individuals have achieved what they have by overcoming a dreadful disadvantage that the rest of us are lucky not to have to endure. Rather, I hope our viewers reflect on the fact that these outstanding people have been ennobled and strengthened by the tremendous challenges they have faced.

In 1992, MDA, which has grown over the past four decades into one of the world's leading voluntary health agencies, established a personal achievement awards program to demonstrate to the nation that the distinctive qualities of people with disabilities are by no means confined to the famous. What could have been more appropriate or timely in that year of the implementation of the 1990 Americans with Disabilities Act than to take an action that could perhaps finally achieve the alteration of public perception of disability, which MDA had struggled over four decades to achieve?

On Labor Day, 1992, it was my privilege to introduce to America MDA's inaugural national personal achievement award winner, Steve Mikita, assistant attorney general of the state of Utah. Stave graduated magna cum laude from Duke University as its first wheelchair student in history and was subsequently named the outstanding young lawyer of the year by the Utah Bar Association. After he spoke on the Telethon with an eloquence that caused phones to light up from coast to coast, people asked me where he had been all this time and why they had not known of him before, so deeply impressed were they by him. I answered that he and thousands like him have been here all along. We just have not adequately *noticed* them.

It is my fervent hope that we can eliminate indifference once and for all and make it possible for all of our fellow citizens with disabilities to gain their rightfully high place in our society.

ON FACING CHALLENGES

John Callahan

I was paralyzed for life in 1972, at the age of 21. A friend and I were driving in a Volkswagen on a hot July night, when he smashed the car at full speed into a utility pole. He suffered only minor injuries. But my spinal cord was severed during the crash, leaving me without any feeling from my diaphragm downward. The only muscles I could move were some in my upper body and arms, and I could also extend my fingers. After spending a lot of time in physical therapy, it became possible for me to grasp a pen.

I've always loved to draw. When I was a kid, I made pictures of everything from Daffy Duck (one of my lifelong role models) to caricatures of my teachers and friends. I've always been a people watcher, it seems; and I've always looked at the world in a sort of skewed way. Everything I see just happens to translate immediately into humor. And so, humor has become my way of coping. As the years have gone by, I have developed a tremendous drive to express my humor by drawing cartoons.

The key to cartooning is to put a different spin on the expected, the normal. And that's one reason why many of my cartoons deal with the disabled: amputees, quadriplegics, paraplegics, and the blind. The public is not used to seeing them in cartoons.

But there's another reason why my subjects are often disabled men and women. I'm sick and tired of people who presume to speak for the disabled. Call me a cripple, call me a gimp, call me paralyzed for life. Just don't call me something I'm not. I'm not "differently abled," and my cartoons show that disabled people should not be treated any differently than anyone else.

All of the men, women, and children who are profiled in the Great Achievers series share this in common: their various handicaps have not prevented them from accomplishing great things. Their life stories are worth knowing about because they have found the strength and courage to develop their talents and to follow their dreams as fully as they can.

Whether able-bodied or disabled, a person must strive to overcome obstacles. There's nothing greater than to see a person who faces challenges and conquers them, regardless of his or her limitations.

Beethoven's confidence shines through in this portrait, painted before 1800. Not yet 30, the composer had already begun to shed the conventions of his contemporaries and establish his own musical voice.

1

TRIUMPH BECOMES TRAGEDY

THE STAGECOACH RIDE from the German town of Bonn to the Austrian city of Vienna was rough and dusty, but in 1787 it was the only way to cross such a great distance. At age 17, Ludwig van Beethoven did not have a great deal of experience in traveling; other than a boyhood trip to Holland, the young musician had not ventured far beyond the small, sleepy towns dotting the Rhine River near his native Bonn.

Thanks to his music teacher, the composer Christian Gottlob Neefe, young Beethoven was able to make the journey to Vienna to study music. A quiet, thin man, Neefe had first recommended that his pupil be offered the opportunity to visit Austria in 1783, in a report he had written for the periodical *Magazin der Muzik*. Neefe had penned the article after Beethoven published his first musical compositions, Three Sonatas for Clavier, at the tender age of 11.

"This youthful genius is deserving of help to enable him to travel," Neefe wrote. "He would surely become a second Wolfgang Amadeus Mozart were he to continue as he has begun."

The wishes of Beethoven's kind teacher finally became a reality in 1787 when Maximilian Franz, the elector (ruler) of Cologne, granted him permission and, most likely, the funds to go to Vienna. At the time, traveling was an extremely costly venture. Because Beethoven's family struggled financially, he could not afford the trip without the aid of a benefactor, even if he used the least expensive means of travel—the public stagecoach—and slept in the most modest lodgings.

Beethoven's journey began in mid-March and took more than two weeks to complete. By day he admired the lush countryside of Austria and of what is today Germany. He had dinner and spent his nights in comfortable country inns. Little did he know, as he raced by the pastoral landscapes, that he would eventually become one of the world's greatest composers. Likewise, as the percussion of hoofbeats lulled him to sleep, Beethoven could not have guessed that, by the age of 50, he would lose his hearing completely.

He had planned on staying in Vienna to study intensively with Wolfgang Amadeus Mozart, the renowned composer to whom his teacher had likened him. A child prodigy, Mozart had gone on to become a prolific composer, and the world revered his musical genius. The biographer Otto Jahn wrote of Mozart and Beethoven's first encounter in his book *W. A. Mozart*:

> Beethoven . . . was taken to Mozart and at the musician's request played something for him which he, taking it for granted was a show-piece prepared for the occasion, praised in a rather cool manner. Beethoven, observing this, begged Mozart to give him a theme for improvisation. He always played admirably when excited, and now he was inspired, too, by the presence of the master whom he reverenced greatly; he played in such a style that Mozart, whose attention and interest grew more and more, finally went silently to some friends who were sitting in an adjoining room, and said, vivaciously, "Keep

Beethoven grew up in this house in Bonn, then the picturesque capital of the Electorate of Cologne.

your eyes on him; someday he will give the world something to talk about."

Mozart did provide Beethoven with a few lessons, but their relationship never solidified. Because Mozart was absorbed by his composition of the opera *Don Giovanni* and was plagued by worries about his father's failing health and his own dwindling finances, he did not prove to be as accessible a teacher as Beethoven would have liked.

Almost immediately after his arrival in Vienna, Beethoven received word from his father that his mother's tuberculosis had worsened and that she was dying. He requested that Beethoven return to Bonn at once. Determined to reach his mother before she died, Beethoven left Vienna without delay, abandoning, for the time, his own dreams of becoming a successful composer.

"For the nearer I came to my native town," Beethoven wrote to Dr. Joseph Wilhelm von Schaden, an acquaintance whom he met in Augsburg, "the more frequently did I receive from my father letters urging me to travel more quickly than usual, because my mother was not in very good health. So I made as much haste as I could," he continued, "the more so as I myself began to feel ill. My yearning to see my ailing mother once more swept all obstacles aside so far as I was concerned, and enabled me to overcome the greatest difficulties." Fortunately, Beethoven reached his mother's bedside in time. Maria Magdalena Beethoven died of consumption on July 17, 1787, at the age of 40.

Beethoven's trip to Vienna had turned out to be a dismal failure. Although his journey abroad was made possible through years of painstaking preparation and by generous monetary contributions, the young musician's stay lasted less than two weeks. Years later, in a letter to Franz Joseph Haydn, a distinguished composer who was to eventually become Beethoven's teacher, Elector Maximilian Franz pointed out that the youth's excursion brought back to Bonn "nothing but debts."

The tragic death of Beethoven's mother proved to be only the beginning of an emotionally trying period for the young composer. The family's financial situation continued to disintegrate. In the weeks before the death of his wife, Beethoven's father, Johann, had written a petition to the elector, who employed him as a court musician, asking for monetary assistance. (It is not known if this request was ever granted.) According to Cäcilia Fischer, a childhood friend of Beethoven's, Johann sold his wife's beautiful wardrobe to a peddler not long after her death, because he needed the money.

Several months later, another tragedy occurred. Beethoven's one-and-a-half-year-old sister, Maria Margarethe, died on November 25.

During this sad time, Beethoven's days overflowed with anguish and poverty. Johann had a reputation for drinking to excess, and the deaths of Maria Magdalena and Maria

Margarethe exacerbated his problem.

Because Beethoven was the oldest son, he suffered the greatest consequences of his father's alcoholism. After his mother's death, he became the unspoken head of the family, taking over the management of the household and assuming responsibility for the financial support of his two adolescent brothers, Kaspar Anton Karl and Nikolaus Johann.

Beethoven also shouldered the role of family disciplinarian, but it was his father, not his younger siblings, who required the most supervision. On one occasion, Johann became so drunk and disorderly that the police threatened to take him into custody. When Beethoven tried to intervene, he too was threatened with arrest.

Eventually, Johann's drinking became so crippling that he could no longer perform his duties as court musician.

This drawing depicts Beethoven's first appearance before the great Austrian composer Wolfgang Amadeus Mozart and other members of Vienna's musical elite. Upon hearing Beethoven improvise on a theme he had given him, Mozart remarked to friends, "Keep your eyes on him; someday he will give the world something to talk about."

Realizing the severity of the situation—Beethoven was now tacitly responsible for the upbringing of his brothers—he wrote to the elector asking that his father's salary be continued, despite the fact that Johann's alcoholism had essentially rendered him useless to the orchestra. The 19-year-old asked that he be permitted to oversee his father's funds.

The elector approved the petition on November 20, 1789, with the provision that Beethoven's father "withdraw to a small city in the Electorate." This threat of banishment, however, was correctly interpreted by Johann as merely a warning; he lived out the rest of his days in Bonn.

His successful petition offered Beethoven little solace. His days were marked by the constant anxiety of overseeing his siblings and of witnessing his father's mental and physical decline. "Since my return to Bonn I have as yet enjoyed very few happy hours," he wrote to Joseph Wilhelm von Schaden. "I have been suffering from melancholia."

While struggling to weather his domestic misfortunes, Beethoven continued his work as a court musician. He participated in the performances of various operas as a member of the orchestra, sometimes playing viola. In order to supplement his income, he also gave music lessons to a handful of pupils, although he did not enjoy teaching.

Contributing to his gloomy situation, young Beethoven could not form a love relationship. He consistently pursued women who were engaged to or involved with other men. His first amorous interest, a beautiful blonde named Jeannette d'Honrath, already admired an Austrian officer. Beethoven revered his student Maria Anna von Westerholt, but she married a member of the nobility in 1792. He carried on a flirtation with Eleonore von Breuning, whom he nicknamed "Adorable Eleonore," but she later married his friend Franz Gerhard Wegeler.

Despite his misfortune in love, Beethoven did enjoy many friendships during his last years in Bonn. He was

The autograph book Beethoven's friends bought for him before his second journey to Vienna. The book is open to the page on which Count Ferdinand von Waldstein wrote, "[Y]ou shall receive <u>Mozart's spirit from Haydn's hands.</u>"

extremely close to fellow members of the court orchestra, and he also spent a good deal of time with his more intimate friends, including Wegeler, the brothers Gerhard and Karl Kügelgen, and the brothers Christoph, Lorenz, and Stephan von Breuning. Many of Beethoven's evenings were spent at the Zehrgarten, a tavern with an adjacent bookshop located near the university. In 1789 he attended a few courses at the university with his two friends Karl Kügelgen and Anton Reicha, although it is not known which subjects he studied.

Although he endured numerous mental hardships during this time, Beethoven could still compose music; it was, more than likely, an emotional outlet. Later in the year, Beethoven enjoyed an explosion of creative energy that would flourish for the next four years. His compositions included piano and chamber music (music composed for performance in a small room or small concert hall by a group of musicians, usually a quartet, with one player for each part), groups of variations (different versions of a principal melody, or theme, within a composition), a piano trio, and a number of songs. Several of the titles, including

"Elegy on the Death of a Poodle" and "The Test of Kissing," reveal the sentimental inclinations of the young composer.

One song, "Feuerfarbe" (Color of Fire), was composed using the words of a poem written by Johann Cristoph Friedrich von Schiller, a well-known dramatist, poet, and writer whom Beethoven admired. A friend of Beethoven's sent the composition to Schiller's wife, Charlotte, with a note stating that the young musician's talents were "universally praised" and that Beethoven was considering setting Schiller's "Ode to Joy" to music. (Beethoven eventually did put the poem to music, but not until 1800, almost 10 years later.)

Although the years 1789 to 1792 proved productive for Beethoven, he still struggled to forge his own musical style. His compositions yielded to the traditional fashion of the Enlightenment, a philosophical movement of the 18th century that emphasized the use of reason, or a person's natural facilities, to examine accepted doctrines and traditions. During this period, many philosophers ridiculed the concepts of miracles, revelations, and mysteries, because these ideas were not rational. This practice of rationalism also applied to the arts. Conventionally organized, Beethoven's early pieces sounded pleasing to the ear, uncluttered, and polite—in other words, rational. Occasionally, the trained musician could detect an exceptional few bars of music or an intriguing variation, but on the whole, these compositions were merely Beethoven's warm-up for the great works to come.

In 1792 France declared war on Austria, and the tranquility of the Electorate of Cologne became merely a memory. The townspeople could hear artillery practice in the distance, and the intimidating strains of the military band drowned out Beethoven's beloved chamber music.

Beethoven craved a change in his life, far away from his father's alcoholism and all of the unpleasantness Bonn held for him. Because his brothers were now old enough to care for themselves, he decided to set out for Vienna once again, this time to study with Franz Joseph Haydn, an esteemed Austrian composer. The second trip was also funded by Maximilian Franz. Neefe, his former teacher, faithfully recorded Beethoven's departure in another musical periodical, *Berliner Musik Zeitung.* "Ludwig van Beethoven . . . went to Vienna at the expense of our Elector to visit Haydn," he wrote, "in order to perfect himself under his direction more fully in the art of composition."

Between October 24 and November 1, 1792, the week before Beethoven departed on his second trip to Vienna, several of his friends pooled their money and bought him an autograph album. In it, they collected the warm sentiments of 15 of his closest companions. His longtime friend Count Ferdinand von Waldstein had lofty hopes for his chum. "With the help of assiduous labor," he wrote, "you shall receive <u>Mozart's spirit from Haydn's hands.</u>" (Mozart had died in Vienna on December 6, 1791.)

With good wishes and a portfolio of numerous musical compositions, Beethoven left Bonn by stagecoach early on the morning of November 2. Now adept at managing money, he carried a ledger in which he recorded his expenses.

The repercussions of war, however, tainted his trip. At one point during his journey, the stagecoach driver risked punishment and drove through a road swarming with army troops from the German principality of Hesse. Beethoven noted the driver's tip in the ledger along with his rationale for proffering it: "because the fellow drove us like the Devil, at the risk of a beating, right through the Hessian army."

After finishing his studies with Haydn, Beethoven intended to return to Bonn, where he would assume a preeminent position in the town's musical life. This plan, however, did not materialize. Beethoven never saw his hometown again.

The title page from Beethoven's first published work, Three Sonatas for Clavier, which he composed at the age of 11.

2

A Musical Legacy

IN THE 18TH century, Germany, as it is known today, did not exist. The world's 20 million German-speaking people were spread among 300 separate states, each of which had its own ruler, currency, army, and regional attire.

The Electorate of Cologne was one of these states. Together with many other principalities in western and central Europe, it made up the Holy Roman Empire, which in theory united church (the Catholic Church, led by the pope in Rome) and state (ruled by the emperor). Historians trace the beginning of the empire to 800 A.D., when the Frankish king Charlemagne was crowned emperor of the Romans by Pope Leo III, or to 962, when the Saxon king Otto I was crowned by Pope John XII. By the 18th century, however, the Holy Roman Empire existed in name only. Years of squabbling between the papacy and the emperors had undermined the supposed spiritual foundations of the empire. And because each prince had complete sovereignty in his own territory, the emperor's authority was largely nonexistent.

Beethoven's birthplace, the scenic little town of Bonn, with about

10,000 inhabitants, was Cologne's capital. Dotted with inns, well-tended gardens, and lush trees, Bonn's quaint streets provided a picturesque setting for the sumptuous Electoral Palace.

Archduke Maximilian Friedrich, the elector at the time of Beethoven's birth, was known as "the fattest man in Europe." He loved music, one of the major forms of entertainment during this period, and especially admired Mozart. He sponsored a court orchestra, partly to indulge his passion for music, and partly to impress upon guests that his court was prosperous.

The name "van Beethoven" is of Dutch-Belgian origin, not German, as is often presumed when the particle "van" appears. In German surnames, "von" usually indicates an aristocratic family lineage. In Dutch surnames, however, the particle "van" is fairly commonplace, comparable to "Mc" and "Mac" in many Irish and Scottish names. Still, throughout his life, Beethoven often put on airs, purporting to be of royal descent.

Beethoven did not exactly choose to become a musician and composer; he essentially inherited his musical career. In the 18th century, the practice of passing down a profession from generation to generation was fairly common. Consequently, when Ludwig van Beethoven was born in Bonn on December 16, 1770, he was already destined to follow in the footsteps of his father and grandfather, both of whom were employed as court musicians.

His grandfather, also named Ludwig van Beethoven, had become an accomplished bass singer and the well-respected *Kapellmeister* (conductor of an orchestra or choir) at the Electoral Court in Bonn, after he moved from Liége, Belgium, in 1733. His substantial responsibilities included overseeing all music performed at banquets, serenades, theatrical events, ballets, and balls, as well as interviewing candidates for employment in the electoral musical service. In 1761 the Court Calendar listed him as one of the 28 *hommes de chambres honoraires* (honorary

Maria Magdalena Laym Beethoven, Beethoven's mother, viewed life as "a chain of sorrows." She died of tuberculosis at age 40.

men of the court), a title the elector conveyed only to extremely accomplished and esteemed men.

Although Beethoven's father, Johann, was not as gifted a musician as Beethoven's grandfather, he did demonstrate above-average musical talents. A tenor singer and a teacher of piano, violin, and voice, Johann also worked as a musician at the Electoral Court. Because of his less-than-stellar musical ability and unpleasant disposition, however, the court did not consider Johann a particularly valuable employee. An official report written in 1784 summed up the court's opinion of him: "Johann Beethoven has a very stale voice, has been long in the service, very poor, of fair deportment and married."

Court organist Christian Gottlob Neefe, who took over Beethoven's musical education when the boy was 10, quickly recognized his pupil's extraordinary talent.

On the other hand, Beethoven's mother, Maria Magdalena Laym, a cook's daughter, enjoyed a favorable reputation. Clever, well spoken, and well respected, she had a serious, practical disposition.

Maria's life overflowed with tragedy. At age 21, when she married Johann, she was already a widow; her first husband, whom she had married when she was just 17, died before her 19th birthday. Not surprisingly, Maria rarely smiled.

Described as "slim and beautiful," Maria bore seven children, but only three survived to adulthood. Her first son, Ludwig Maria, was christened on April 2, 1769, and died six days later. The following year, she gave birth to the second Ludwig, who would survive to become a famous composer. Both Kaspar Anton Karl, christened on April 8, 1774, and Nikolaus Johann, christened on October 2, 1776, also lived to adulthood. But Anna Maria Franziska, born in 1779, lived for only a few days; Franz Georg, born in 1781, lived two years; and Maria Margarethe died in 1787, at the age of one and a half. Although infant mortality was much more common during Beethoven's time than it is today, the grief that comes with the loss of a child was probably no less painful.

Maria also suffered greatly from her husband's alcoholism. Johann often left her at home alone, and she fretted over his drinking debts, which began to accumulate to an alarming degree. When asked to advise a young neighbor and friend of Beethoven's, Cäcilia Fischer, regarding a suitor, Maria's remarks about marriage expressed her own bitterness.

"What is marriage?" she asked. "A little joy, and then a chain of sorrows."

On the surface, young Ludwig possessed a cheerful demeanor. He loved to romp outdoors in the garden of the palace, and he especially enjoyed being carried piggyback by his cousins. He delighted in playing jokes on unsuspecting neighbors and friends. Once, a neighbor caught the boy stealing eggs from her henhouse. She did not punish him but merely laughed and called him a fox.

"I am more of a music fox than a hen fox," the young composer replied.

But even at a young age, Ludwig shared his mother's "chain of sorrows." Although his personality sparkled, he also exhibited serious moods and bouts of shyness. Cäcilia Fischer lived along the Bonngasse River and owned two telescopes. Beethoven often sequestered himself in her attic and spent hours looking through the telescopes over the Rhine at the Seven Mountains, daydreaming, lost in his own imagination.

According to Cäcilia, her friend often neglected his personal hygiene. She even confronted him about his shabby appearance once.

"Why do you look so dirty?" she asked. "You should make yourself proper."

"When I grow up, nobody will care about it," he responded.

Beethoven's musical education began at age five; Johann taught his son the rudiments of the clavier (an instrument similar to a piano) and the violin. But Johann lacked patience and often used corporal punishment and verbal abuse when the boy's performance did not match his expectations. Those who witnessed these lessons agreed they were exercises in cruelty and excessive strictness.

Head Burgomaster Windeck remembered the young Ludwig van Beethoven "standing in front of the clavier and weeping." Cäcilia recalled him as "a tiny boy, standing on a little footstool in front of the clavier, to which the implacable severity of his father had so early condemned him." A childhood companion stated that "Beethoven's father used violence when it came to making him start his musical studies, and there were few days when he was not beaten in order to compel him to set himself at the piano." "He treated him harshly," Court Councillor Krupp wrote in a letter, "and sometimes shut him up in the cellar."

Later, Johann engaged the services of another musician, Tobias Pfeiffer, to supplement his son's education. During his appointment, Pfeiffer stayed with the Beethovens, and in the evenings, he often visited local taverns with Johann. Bernhard Mäurer, a cellist who played in Bonn at the time, observed that

> often, when Pfeiffer had been boozing with Ludwig's father in a wine-tavern until 11 or 12 o'clock, he went home with him where [they found] Ludwig in bed sleeping. The father roughly shook him awake, the boy gathered his wits and, weeping, went to the piano where he remained, with Pfeiffer seated next to him, until morning.

Although he disciplined Ludwig with extraordinary severity, Johann also expressed great love for his son. He spoke of Beethoven as his "only joy" and predicted, correctly, that "someday he'll be a great man of the world."

Despite his early distaste for his rigorous music lessons, Beethoven did display exceptional musical talents. Partly because his finances were in such a poor state, Johann took advantage of his son's remarkable ability. He invited audiences in Bonn and from the court to come to his house to hear Beethoven play, often charging admission. In 1778 he presented his six-year-old son at a concert in Cologne.

Although he seemed to harbor ulterior motives, Johann's primary goal was probably to equip his son with the skills needed to earn a decent living. But early on, Beethoven preferred improvisation on the clavier to formal music lessons. He spent a good bit of time experimenting with chords and the placement of notes.

Johann discouraged his son's inventions. Once, when the boy composed a tune with chords on the piano, Johann rebuked and threatened him.

"More of that fooling around?" he said. "Go away, or I'll box your ears."

In addition to his musical instruction, Beethoven also attended school. Unfortunately, no documents exist that can confirm the exact length of his study. Formal educa-

A portrait of Beethoven at age 13. Around this time he was appointed deputy court organist.

tion was mandatory in Bonn, so Beethoven probably attended between the ages of 6 and 11, which was the normal duration of elementary education. His courses included reading, writing, mathematics, religion, choral singing, and Latin.

Beethoven made little progress at school, with mathematics proving to be his most difficult subject. In fact, he never learned to do arithmetic other than simple addition or subtraction problems. Later, when Beethoven was in his 50s, his nephew attempted to teach him the multiplication tables, to no avail. Throughout his life, math remained a mystery to the composer.

Beethoven was not a talented writer, either. His letters and manuscripts overflowed with misspelled words, clichés, and grandiose language. Beethoven explained why he did not enjoy writing in a letter to his friend Franz Wegeler. "I often compose the answer in my mind, but when I wish to write it down, I usually throw the pen away, because I cannot write as I feel." As he grew older, his spelling deteriorated even further, and his handwriting became frenzied, almost to the point of illegibility.

But Beethoven did have a flair for languages, demonstrating a basic command of Latin, French, and Italian. (The instructions on sheet music are traditionally written in Italian.) He also developed a passion for reading, studying the works of the poets Homer and Virgil and the biographer Plutarch.

Although as a young boy he studied music at his father's insistence, Beethoven gradually grew to love music on his own, probably because his talents won praise and attention from Johann as well as from other adults.

After years of assiduous practice, Beethoven finally acquired finesse and character as a musician. By the time he entered his second decade, he considered himself to be his father's equal in musical ability, and he began to compose.

The court organist Christian Gottlob Neefe became Beethoven's teacher in 1780 or 1781 when the boy was 10, and Beethoven's genius blossomed under his tutelage. His teaching style contrasted sharply to Pfeiffer's. Instead of rudely waking Beethoven in the middle of the night to practice, for example, Neefe taught him during normal hours and demonstrated patience and encouragement. Neefe recognized his pupil's talents and motivated him. He supported Beethoven's early stabs at composition and helped to facilitate the publication of three of his early compositions, Sonatas for Clavier, which he composed at age 11.

Thanks to recommendations from his kind and enthusiastic teacher, Beethoven embarked on a promising career
as a musician in 1782. He served as assistant court organist and, the next year, as cembalist (harpsichord player).
Although he did not receive a salary for these two brief
tenures, they furnished him with practical professional
experience.

In 1784 Beethoven was officially appointed as deputy
court organist and received a salary of 150 gulden (about
$750) per year. Although his position might seem impres-
sive by today's standards, during the 1780s it was not
uncommon for a youth to serve as a musical apprentice.

Most musicians of the late 18th century wore uniforms,
and Beethoven was no exception. His elegant garb consisted of a "sea-green dresscoat, green short buckled
trousers, silk stockings white or black, a waistcoat of
white flowered silk with flap piping of real gold, hair
curled and with a pigtail, a collapsible hat carried under
the left arm, a sword with a silver strap on the left side."
Court musicians were the only exception to the law against
musicians carrying swords.

Because of his dark complexion, Beethoven acquired
the nickname *der Spagnol* (the Spaniard). He had broad
shoulders, a short neck, and a large head. His dark, wavy
hair and distinct sideburns framed his serious, full face.
Although he displayed confidence with respect to his
musical abilities, his gait—stooped and bent forward
slightly at the waist—revealed an unsure teenager, going
through the awkward tribulations of adolescence and a
tumultuous home life.

When Beethoven settled in Vienna in the early 1790s, the city was one of Europe's fore-most cultural centers. The domed building to the right of center is the Imperial Palace; the building at the far right is the Burgtheater.

3

THE DIFFICULT PUPIL

LIKE MOST CITIES during Beethoven's time, Vienna had two sides. The sumptuous neighborhoods that housed the city's wealthiest citizens and architectural treasures were prominently located in the center of town. The Church of St. Stephen; the Neuer Markt, an Italian-style square; and the Hofburg, a complex of palaces where the newly crowned Emperor Franz II now resided, were all situated within a few blocks of each other, like a cluster of jewels.

The less glamorous wards remained hidden within the center of the city. There, the impoverished Viennese dwelled in dilapidated buildings located on dank, narrow streets where mortality rates for tuberculosis, dysentery, and typhus soared. In coffee houses illuminating these shabby neighborhoods, the workers congregated, read newspapers, and talked of current events in slangy German.

Vienna's special character came largely from the fact that its citizens—rich, middle class, and poor—loved spectacle and entertainment. In his book *Travels into Different Parts of Europe, in the Years 1791 and 1792,* John Owen wrote that "good cheer is, indeed, pursued here in every quarter, and mirth is worshipped in every form."

The townsfolk gathered on street corners and in public squares to watch acrobats, musicians, jugglers, and puppeteers perform. Dancing was a popular activity, and people from all walks of life congregated in ballrooms, often wearing masks in order to make this commingling of classes socially acceptable. Theaters and music halls played an especially important part in Viennese daily life.

Beethoven arrived in Vienna on November 10, 1792, to study composition. He continued to diligently record all of his expenditures and to budget the small stipend that he received from Archduke Maximilian Franz. According to his records, he spent money on rent, the lease of a piano, meals, a cleaning woman, wood, clothing, and a desk.

On December 18, 1792, scarcely seven weeks after Beethoven had departed from Bonn, his father died after a long illness. The exact cause of his death is unknown, but the official reason is listed as heart failure. Few people mourned him, and Archduke Maximilian Franz offered little sympathy, stating callously that "the revenues from the liquor tax" would dwindle as a result of Johann Beethoven's passing.

While preparing to leave for Vienna, Beethoven had almost certainly known of his father's impending death. But he had departed anyway, perhaps because he could not bear to witness the death of another family member or perhaps as an act of defiance.

One of the first people Beethoven visited in Vienna was probably Franz Joseph Haydn, the renowned composer under whom he was to study. Vienna beamed with pride over Haydn. Not only was he esteemed as one of Europe's most respected and talented composers, but he was also admired for his personality. He exuded an air of humor and aristocracy.

When the lessons began, Haydn used the music textbook *Gradus ad Parnassum,* and, with great enthusiasm, Beethoven composed pieces based upon chants outlined in

Franz Joseph Haydn, Vienna's most beloved composer, became Beethoven's teacher in 1792. Their relationship proved tumultuous: Haydn became irritated by his pupil's headstrong insistence on developing his own musical style, and Beethoven, for his part, believed that Haydn envied his talent and was indifferent to his progress.

this book. But Haydn hardly seemed to be an attentive teacher. Of the 245 existing compositions Beethoven created during this time, only 42 show corrections or changes made by Haydn. (Haydn might have corrected Beethoven's errors verbally, however.)

From the beginning, the relationship between Haydn and Beethoven proved tumultuous. Haydn asked that Beethoven identify his status as a "pupil of Haydn" on the title page of all of his works of composition. But Beethoven, who was desperately trying to forge his own identity as a composer, adamantly refused, much to Haydn's chagrin.

After a few months of instruction, Beethoven sensed

Prince Karl Lichnowsky, one of Beethoven's earliest patrons and a lifelong friend.

that Haydn felt jealous of his talents and indifferent about his development as a musician. In early 1793, scarcely six months after Beethoven began lessons with Haydn, he sought to study in secret with another teacher, Johann Schenk.

At an initial meeting with Schenk, Beethoven improvised on the piano and then showed him the exercises in counterpoint (composing musical material above or below the main melody line) that he had worked on with Haydn. According to Schenk, these exercises "disclosed the fact that there were mistakes in every mode." Many errors Beethoven had made under Haydn's instruction remained uncorrected, and in some cases, when he did amend a mistake, he made another one in the process.

Schenk remedied these drills and suggested that Beethoven recopy them in his own handwriting to disguise the fact that he was studying with another teacher. But a rival musician and one of Vienna's most successful pianists, Abbé Joseph Gelinek, soon uncovered his secret. When Gelinek and Beethoven quarreled, Gelinek told Haydn about Beethoven's covert studies.

In 1793 Beethoven virtually ceased composing except for the formal exercises he completed. This was probably because it had been an extremely stressful year: his father had died, he had moved to a strange city, and he was not making what he considered to be sufficient progress in his studies with his music teacher.

Haydn prepared to leave for London in January 1794 and arranged for Beethoven to study with another teacher, Johann Georg Albrechtsberger, the Kapellmeister of St. Stephen's Church. Although Albrechtsberger seemed to get along with Beethoven very well, he informed a fellow musician that Beethoven's work was "trash" and that "he learned absolutely nothing and will never accomplish anything decent." Beethoven respected Albrechtsberger's course of study—going "back to the basics"—but he assessed him as a "musical pedant" and a composer of "musical skeletons." Beethoven studied with Albrechts-berger until the spring of 1795.

Meanwhile, Beethoven's brother Karl moved to Vienna in 1794. He taught music for a short time, then obtained a position as a bank cashier in the state offices.

Antonio Salieri, the Imperial Kapellmeister and director of Vienna's opera house, also taught Beethoven, though less regularly than his other instructors. Salieri treated Beethoven kindly and, of all his teachers in Vienna, had the most profound influence on Beethoven's style. He also trained Beethoven in vocal and dramatic composition.

Salieri once criticized one of Beethoven's composi-tions, saying that it was not appropriate for the mood he was attempting to convey. But the next day, he confessed to his pupil, "I can't get your melody out of my head."

"Then, Mr. Salieri," Beethoven responded wryly, "it cannot have been so utterly bad."

As his competence in the classical techniques of com-position and theory improved, Beethoven began to express his creativity with more confidence. All his teachers, espe-cially Salieri and Albrechtsberger, criticized him for being too headstrong and independent; he preferred indulging his own inventiveness to strictly following the exercises they showed him. Haydn declared that Beethoven's first compositions "pleased me very much; but I will confess that I do not understand the later ones. It seems to me that he writes more and more fantastically." As his skill and conviction grew, Beethoven time and again shed the skins of his teachers so that he could assert his own voice as a composer.

Beethoven's disregard for his personal appearance changed little from his boyhood. Because he found shav-ing a difficult operation, nicks and cuts usually dotted his face. Short of stature, pockmarked, and clumsy, he was commonly described as "ugly." The composer Luigi Cherubini used more diplomatic terms, calling him "an unlicked bear."

Prone to temper tantrums, Beethoven once flung an unacceptable meal at a waiter's head. Another time, he threw eggs at a housekeeper because they were not fresh. After these episodes, Beethoven usually felt remorseful and apologized for his behavior.

Beethoven's friends, however, brought out his more pleasant qualities. He loved to joke and laugh, and he enjoyed playing charades and forfeits. He liked going to the theater and to the opera. He relished nature and took daily walks in the Vienna woods or along the Danube River.

But it was Beethoven's genius as a musician—not his appearance or personality—that won him the popularity and recognition he craved. Prince Karl Lichnowsky, who lived in the same building as Beethoven on the Alser-strasse (a street), admired Beethoven so much that he invited the composer to live with him "as a member of the family" in 1793. Beethoven stayed with the Lichnowskys until May 1795.

Lichnowsky and his wife, Princess Christiane (who was one of Vienna's most talented pianists), developed a deep affection for Beethoven. The couple recognized and nurtured the composer's creativity, sometimes with constructive criticism.

A lover of music and a competent pianist himself, Prince Lichnowsky hosted parties every Friday evening and provided chamber music for his guests' entertainment. Soon, Beethoven began playing at these informal gatherings, and he gained a reputation in Vienna as a virtuoso pianist.

It was not long before Prince Lichnowsky replaced Archduke Maximilian Franz as Beethoven's patron. When the elector terminated Beethoven's salary, Lichnowsky provided him with a yearly sum of 600 thalers (about $5,100) as long as he remained unemployed. In 1795, when Beethoven began once again to compose, Prince Lichnowsky arranged to have his Opus 1 (the Three Piano

Trios) published. Beethoven also composed "Adelaide," the first two Piano Concertos, no. 2, and a variety of smaller works and chamber music, including Six Minuets for Orchestra, Twelve German Dances for Orchestra, and Twelve Minuets for Orchesra.

On March 29 and 30, 1795, Beethoven appeared in public for the first time as a piano virtuoso and composer. He performed at two concerts in the Burgtheater, given to benefit widows and orphans of the Society of Musicians. During the first concert, "Ludwig *von* Beethoven" presented what is now known as his Second Piano Concerto. During the second concert, he "improvised on the pianoforte [piano]." A few days later, *Wiener Zeitung,* a leading Vienna newspaper, reported that "the famous Herr Ludwig von Beethoven reaped wholehearted approval of the public." The fact that his performance and his published music were well accepted inspired Beethoven's creativity even further.

In 1796 Beethoven embarked on a five-month tour of Prague and Berlin, and the audiences received his music with enthusiasm. He played an entire evening for the elector of Saxony, who later presented him with a gold snuffbox. In Berlin he performed several times at the court of Frederick William II, the king of Prussia.

Although the year proved successful for Beethoven, it was the beginning of calamity for Austria. Napoléon Bonaparte, a general of the French revolutionary army, led an offensive into northern Italy (then a province of Austria) and won a series of battles. After claiming other republics and such cities as Milan, Modena, Ferrara, and Bologna for France, he conquered the lower portion of Austria in 1797.

The Austrians, who wanted peace with France, signed the Treaty of Campo Formio on October 17, 1797. The treaty stipulated that Austria give up parts of her territory in the Netherlands and Lombardy and allow France to freely navigate the Rhine River.

A page from the score of the Sonata in the Manner of a Fantasy *(now better known as the* Moonlight Sonata), *which Beethoven dedicated to Giulietta Guicciardi (opposite page), his attractive 16-year-old student. Though Beethoven was thoroughly captivated by Guicciardi, her higher social class stood in the way of a possible marriage.*

Although Beethoven composed Three Violin Sonatas Opus 12, *Pathétique* Sonata Opus 13, and Two Piano Sonatas Opus 14 in 1799, the joy of composition was tainted by the 28-year-old's first symptoms of deafness. Despite his fears, he kept his affliction a secret from everyone except his doctors, and he continued to compose and perform.

In 1800 Beethoven accepted a large salary from Prince Lichnowsky. He gave a concert in April, again at the Burgtheater—the first for the promotion of his own music (and finances). He performed the Septet, the First Symphony, and the Piano Concerto Opus 15. Even though the reviews were lukewarm at best, the concert symbolized his acceptance as a major composer.

The First Symphony gained recognition throughout Austria and the German states. Nevertheless, it angered many music critics. One called it "the outrageous effron-

tery of a young man." Another objected to Beethoven's "prodigal use of the most barbaric dissonances [combinations of sounds that are disagreeable to the ear]."

Despite this disapproval, Beethoven continued to perform and to publish music. In 1800 he composed six quartets, Piano Concerto no. 3, and *Creatures of Prometheus,* a ballet score that eventually became successful. (The ballet was performed a total of 23 times between 1801 and 1802.)

By 1801, though, he could no longer contain his despair over his impending deafness. He confessed his condition, via letters, to his two close friends Karl Amenda and Dr. Franz Wegeler.

To Karl Amenda　　　Vienna, July 1, 1801

. . . . How often would I like to have you here with me, for your B[eethoven] is leading a very unhappy life and is at variance with Nature and his Creator. . . . Let me tell you that my most prized possession, <u>my hearing,</u> has greatly deteriorated. When you were still with me, I already felt the symptoms, but I said nothing about them. Now they have become much worse. We must wait and see whether my hearing can be restored.

To Franz Wegeler　　　Vienna, June 19, 1801

. . . . For almost two years I have ceased to attend any social functions, just because I find it impossible to say to people: I am deaf. If I had any other profession I might be able to cope with my infirmity; but in my profession it is a terrible handicap. And if my enemies, of whom I have a fair number, were to hear about it, what would they say?— In order to give you some idea of this strange deafness, let me tell you that in the theater I have to place myself close to the orchestra in order to understand what the actor is saying and that at a distance I cannot hear the high notes of instruments or voices.

Music gave Beethoven some solace, and indeed, this was a period of prolific creation for the composer. In the letter to Wegeler in which he announced his deafness, he also wrote about his productivity.

"I live entirely in my music," he said, "and hardly have I completed one composition when I have already begun another. At my present rate of composing, I often produce three or four works at the same time."

Fortunately for Beethoven, love eased his pain to some degree. He was enamored of one of his students, Countess Giulietta Guicciardi, a pretty 16-year-old with large, dark eyes and curly hair. Beethoven told Wegeler, "[F]or the first time I feel that marriage might bring me happiness. Unfortunately, she is not my class [Giulietta came from a wealthy family], and at the moment I certainly could not marry—I must still bustle about a good deal."

Beethoven admired Giulietta so much that in 1801 he dedicated the *Sonata in the Manner of a Fantasy* to her. It started with a slow, dreamlike movement, followed by a lively (or scherzo) middle. The piece closed dramatically, with a quick, climactic movement. A poet and critic named Ludwig Rellstab renamed it *Moonlight Sonata* in 1832, because the opening movement reminded him of moonlight rippling across water. It is now one of Beethoven's best-known works.

With each passing day, Beethoven's world grew more silent. Although he accepted his deafness with honesty and a reluctant sense of "resignation," he could not envision the myriad of obstacles with which he would eventually have to contend in order to continue composing.

Beethoven walking in the Vienna woods, a favorite pastime. By his early 30s, the composer began to brood about his progressing deafness and to withdraw from social contacts because of it.

4

Learning to Live
in Silence

SOMETIMES BEFORE THEIR morning lesson, Beethoven and his
student Ferdinand Ries walked in the streets and surrounding fields of
Vienna. As Ries later recounted, it was during one of these walks in
1802 that he

> called [Beethoven's] attention to a shepherd who was piping very agree-
> ably in the woods on a flute made of a twig of elder. For a half hour
> Beethoven could hear nothing, and though I assured him it was the same
> with me (which was not the case), he became extremely quiet and
> morose. When occasionally he seemed to be merry, it was generally to
> the extreme of boisterousness; but this happened seldom.

Beethoven's deafness had not, in actuality, progressed very much.
The hearing he had lost up to this point consisted only of the capacity
to distinguish high frequencies and the ability to differentiate words.
More than anything, what troubled him was tinnitus (a sensation
of ringing, humming, or buzzing in the ears). But sudden, loud sounds
also caused him pain. Fortunately, he could still discern music, if

only through vibrations.

Doctors prescribed the most up-to-date remedies, although by today's standards, several of the treatments might sound absurd. Beethoven applied an herbal ointment to his arms, took cold and tepid baths, and tried infusions and pills, but his condition continued to worsen.

His hearing loss drove him into a state of anguish and despair. He felt embarrassed by his affliction and grew so withdrawn and depressed that he contemplated suicide. Because his physician, Dr. Johann Schmidt, ordered Beethoven to protect his ears from loud noises (and probably to help heal his wounded spirit, too), he decided to spend the summer in a quiet place. He moved to the tiny village of Heiligenstadt. From his quarters in a large, pleasant home located on an elevated plain, Beethoven could see miles of sunny, green meadows, the Danube River, and the Carpathian Mountains.

While he stayed in Heiligenstadt, Beethoven took curative baths and walked through the lush fields. But because the village was so far removed from Vienna, Beethoven had a lot of free time to brood about his deafness. In a long letter dated October 1802, now known as the Heiligenstadt Testament, he expressed his grief to his brothers:

> Though born with a fiery, active temperament . . . I was soon compelled to withdraw myself, to live alone. If at times I tried to forget all this, oh how harshly was I flung back by the doubly bad experience of my bad hearing. Yet it was impossible for me to say to people, "Speak louder, shout, for I am deaf." . . . But what a humiliation for me when someone standing next to me heard a flute in the distance and <u>I heard nothing</u>, or someone heard a <u>shepherd singing</u> and again I heard nothing. Such incidents drove me almost to despair; a little more of that and I would have ended my life—it was only my <u>art</u> that held me back. Ah, it seemed to me impossible to leave the world until I had brought forth all that I felt was within me.

Beethoven ended the letter with an emotional statement

to be read and executed after his death:

> Heiligenstadt, October 10th, 1802, thus I bid thee farewell—and indeed sadly.—Yes, that fond hope—which I brought here with me, to a cured degree at least—this I must now wholly abandon. As the leaves of autumn fall and are withered—so likewise my hope has been blighted—I leave here—almost as I came—even the high courage—which often inspired me in the beautiful days of summer—has disappeared—Oh Providence—grant me at last but one day of pure joy—it is so long since real joy echoed in my heart—Oh when—Oh when, Oh Divine One—shall I feel it again in the temple of nature and of mankind—Never?—No—Oh that would be too hard.

The Heiligenstadt Testament reveals many of the powerful emotions—such as remorse, fear, loneliness, and anxiety—that the composer felt during this trying time.

The composer at Heiligenstadt. On the advice of his physician, Beethoven spent the summer of 1802 in the tiny village, where he hoped his hearing might improve. When that hope was dashed, he wrote the famous Heiligenstadt Testament, in which he declared that only his art had prevented him from ending his life.

But in spite of the gloom of his message, Beethoven's passionate nature and his awareness of his own capabilities shine through.

In 1801 Emanuel Schikanader opened an opera house, the Theater-an-der-Wien. This was an ambitious undertaking, since Vienna's other two theaters, the Burgtheater and the Kärntnertor Theater, were already well established and attracting large audiences. Despite the odds, the young entrepreneur succeeded in drawing impressive crowds, largely by engaging lively performers.

One of these performers was Beethoven. After so many years of struggle, his popularity had finally spread across Europe, and audiences now ranked him with Haydn as the greatest of living composers.

Schikanader made Beethoven three generous offers: to compose an opera for the theater, to oversee the theater's orchestra, and to conduct the orchestra whenever he wanted to. Schikanader threw in an added bonus—free lodging in the theater. In 1803 Beethoven moved there, along with his brother Karl, with whom he was especially close during this time.

Beethoven immediately arranged for a concert that consisted solely of his own works. It featured his oratorio, *Christus am Ölberg* (Christ on Mount Olive), Opus 85, which he had composed in March. The *Wiener Zeitung* announced the concert:

> On the 5th of April, Herr Ludwig van Beethoven will produce a new oratorio set to music by him, *Christus am Ölberg,* in the R.I. privil. Theater-an-der-Wien. The other pieces to be performed will be announced on the large billboard.

The final rehearsal took place on the day of the performance, and at 5:00 A.M., Beethoven summoned Ries, his student, to help him with last-minute preparations, which included copying some music. When he arrived at Beethoven's apartment, Ries found Beethoven in bed,

Handwritten title page of the Third Symphony. Beethoven had intended to dedicate the work—which communicated his feelings about heroism—to Napoléon Bonaparte, whose military campaigns, he believed, were leading to a more just order. But after hearing that Napoléon had crowned himself emperor, a furious Beethoven rubbed out the dedication, producing the hole that can be seen on the third staff from the top.

scribbling out music on separate sheets of paper.

The conductor, Ignaz van Seyfried, later commented on the concert:

> In the playing of the concerto movements he asked me to turn the pages for him; but—heaven help me!—that was easier said than done. I saw almost nothing but empty leaves; at the most on one page or the other a few Egyptian hieroglyphics, wholly unintelligible to me scribbled down to serve as clues for him for he played nearly all of the solo part from memory, since, as was often the case, he had not had time enough to put it all down on paper.

Beethoven's new works, however, were not warmly received. One critic reported in the newspaper *Der Freymüthige* that "the two symphonies and single passages in the oratorio were voted very beautiful, but the work in its entirety was too long, too artificial in structure and lacking expressiveness, especially in the vocal parts." The *Zeitung die Elegante Welt* criticized Beethoven for performing "not completely to his public's satisfaction."

After the performance, Beethoven put aside the negative reviews and became obsessed with a new work—the

The Theater-an-der-Wien, where Beethoven was furnished a free apartment and where many of his works were premiered.

Third Symphony. He spent much of the summer of 1803 composing in Oberdöbling. Although he worked long hours, he made time to enjoy his customary morning walks along the Danube Canal and in the town's lush gardens and vineyards.

In November Beethoven began to compose the opera that Schikaneder wanted so desperately. The work, called *Vestal Feuer* (The Vestal Flame), consumed almost all of his time, and by the year's end, he had nearly completed the first scene.

But in February 1804 the theater's ownership changed hands, and the new owners temporarily annulled Beethoven's contract. The owners also asked Beethoven to find new lodgings. He stayed with his friend Stephan von Breuning until the two men quarreled. Then he spent a few weeks in Baden. He even considered moving to Paris because he felt his work would be better appreciated there.

In the meantime, Beethoven continued to work feverishly, revising the Third Symphony, finishing the Triple

Concerto Opus 56, creating the Piano Sonatas Opus 53 and Opus 54, and experimenting on a new idea that became the *Appassionata*. As he composed, he scribbled his ideas in large sketchbooks; his musical notes made long, sweeping lines across the pages.

Beethoven completed the Third Symphony in May 1804. Originally, he had intended to dedicate it to Napoléon, whose military genius he admired and whose restructuring of the French government he supported, believing it to be a step toward a more just system. (The possibility does exist, however, that Beethoven also had an ulterior motive: he might have assumed that the dedication would smooth his passage into revolutionary France.)

The symphony, particularly in the first movement, mimics Beethoven's idealization of Napoléon as a hero: in his composition, Beethoven attempted to set his spiritual feelings to music. This marked a turning point in his work, which had slowly been evolving away from reason and toward emotion.

In the second, adagio (slow) movement, Beethoven expressed his imaginings about death. He must have been successful, because the English poet Samuel Taylor Coleridge called it "a funeral procession in deep purple." Indeed, the composition, which sounds somber and morbid, evokes many sad emotions.

When Beethoven, a lifelong Republican, learned in December 1804 that Napoléon had crowned himself emperor, he was angry and believed he had been betrayed by his hero. "Now, he, too, will trample on all the rights of man and indulge only his ambition," the composer railed. "He will exalt himself above all others and become a tyrant!" Beethoven rubbed out the inscription "Bonaparte," tore the title page in half, and then renamed the symphony *Eroica* (or the *Heroic* Symphony).

Eroica premiered at Prince Lobkowitz's palace before a private gathering. The prince might have recognized the importance of this piece, because he arranged for

Beethoven to perform the symphony at another private performance, one for his esteemed guest, Prince Louis Ferdinand of Prussia. Louis Ferdinand enjoyed it so much that he requested an encore.

The first public performance of the composition occurred at the Theater-an-der-Wien on April 7, 1805. The symphony puzzled many listeners. At once, it sounded scary, compelling, exciting, and fantastic. Beethoven broke many of the symphonic conventions that audiences were used to. For example, he started the piece with two hammer blows, which, in 1805, was extremely unorthodox. At a time when the custom was to use one or two transitional sections between themes within a piece, Beethoven incorporated *three*. And *Eroica* was almost three times the length of any previous symphony. In it, the composer attempted to meld all of the emotional elements of heroism—nobility, strength, fortitude. For this reason, the years 1803–1813 are known as Beethoven's Heroic Decade.

Another innovation of Beethoven's baffled even the most musically knowledgeable listeners. In the first allegro (a quick, lively passage) of the symphony, the horn made a startling entrance. To an untrained ear, it seemed as if the horn player had made a mistake and had come in at the wrong time, even though Beethoven had planned this "surprise."

At the first rehearsal of the symphony, Ries, who was not acquainted with the score, stood next to Beethoven, who conducted. When he heard the horn, he assumed an error had been made.

"Can't that damned hornist count?" he asked. "It sounds infamously false!" According to Ries, Beethoven came close to boxing his ears and "did not forgive the slip for a long time."

The *Eroica* Symphony is an especially significant work because it bridged the two styles of the time. It contains the order and reason characteristic of the Enlightenment and the emotional expressiveness of the Romantic movement.

Romanticism was born in Germany in about 1770 with Sturm und Drang (Storm and Stress), a literary movement whose works depicted the emotional struggles of the individual against the conventional or Classical order of society. It caught on, and the movement spread quickly throughout Europe.

Unlike the followers of the Enlightenment, the Romantics loved nature and felt that emotion and imagination should take precedence over science and logic. They detested and rebelled against social conventions and rules. They also turned their backs on Classical art forms such as measured verse in poetry and glorified portraits in painting.

Although Beethoven did not formally subscribe to these Romantic beliefs, the philosophy of his contemporaries influenced him, and his music eventually became known as the embodiment of Romanticism.

Napoléon Bonaparte, the Corsican-born military genius and emperor of France, decisively defeated Austria in 1805. The French occupation of Vienna brought poverty and hardship, and many of Beethoven's friends and sponsors fled the city.

Beethoven's opera contract was renewed in late 1804, and once again, he took up his apartment at the Theater-an-der-Wien. His residence exuded disorder. Books and music dotted every corner, and leftover bits of food and half-consumed bottles of wine collected on tables. Scribbled works in progress decorated the piano, the desk, and the music stands. Letters speckled the floor.

Beethoven hoped to finish the opera by the end of June 1805, after which he planned to move to Paris. But a pre-occupation with the composition of a new opera, *Leonore* (which he eventually renamed *Fidelio*), combined with a healthy dose of love, persuaded him to remain in Vienna.

Fidelio celebrated, somewhat ideally, the joys of marital love—loyalty, order, understanding, and serenity—as well as brotherhood and triumph over injustice. In it, a seemingly virtuous father, Rocco, tries to bring about the marriage of his daughter, Marcelline, to her sweetheart, Fidelio. But appearances are deceiving. Fidelio is really Leonore in disguise, looking for her husband, Florestan, who is imprisoned in a cell that happens to be just under the very spot on which they are standing. The plot thickens, and Leonore heroically saves her imprisoned husband, to whom she remains faithful.

Beethoven's preoccupation with love can be attributed to Countess Josephine Brunsvik Deym. The year 1804 proved a trying one for the countess. A few weeks after the death of her husband, she gave birth to her fourth child; a few months after that, she suffered a nervous breakdown. When the countess moved in with her family in Vienna, Beethoven, who had been a friend of Josephine's husband, began to visit the Brunsvik house frequently. He gave Josephine piano lessons free of charge.

Beethoven soon became smitten with the beautiful young widow. Although Josephine cherished his friendship, she did not want the relationship to go any further. He composed a song for her, "An die Hoffnung" (To Hope), but upon its publication, Beethoven removed her name from the dedication to spare her embarrassment. Eventually, his letters to her resumed a cool, detached tone. In the fall, Josephine left Vienna. By the end of the year, she was ignoring Beethoven altogether, and another man, Count Wolkenstein, began to woo her.

In November 1805 Napoléon's army occupied Vienna. Only a week later, *Fidelio,* the only opera Beethoven ever completed, premiered at the Theater-an-der-Wien. It proved a most unfortunate time for the debut of an opera: How could the Viennese concentrate on music when their beloved city was in the hands of the French?

Like many of Beethoven's new works, *Fidelio* received unfavorable reviews and was misunderstood. It lacked the unity that audiences were accustomed to and struck them as bizarre and overly long. In the middle of one performance, someone from the audience shouted out, "I'll give another kreuzer [a small coin] if the thing will but stop!" After only three performances, the theater dropped *Fidelio* from its roster.

With the occupation of Austria by the French, Vienna essentially turned upside down. The day after the premiere, the French fired the editor of the *Wiener Zeitung* and replaced him with a new editor who packed the paper with propaganda. General Pierre Augustin Hulin, who served under Napoléon, set up headquarters in the palace of Beethoven's friend Prince Lobkowitz. Many of Beethoven's friends and sponsors fled the city. The new government imposed additional taxes.

Napoléon's invasion did not mark the end of Austria's troubles. On December 2, 1805—the first anniversary of his crowning as emperor—Napoléon moved his army north and obliterated the combined Austrian and Russian forces (led by Emperor Franz II and Emperor Aleksandr II) at Austerlitz, a small town in what was then Moravia. Nearly 15,000 Austrians and Russians were killed and another 20,000 were taken prisoner.

One of Beethoven's "ear trumpets," rudimentary hearing aids designed by the composer's friend Johann Mälzel, photographed atop the manuscript of the Eroica Symphony. *The narrow end was placed in Beethoven's ear, the bell pointed toward the source of the sound.*

5

THE PROLIFIC YEARS

AFTER NAPOLEON'S EXTENSIVE military victories, the Holy
Roman Empire formally dissolved; its principalities were now governed
by France. In August 1806, Emperor Franz II, the last Holy Roman
Emperor, was forced to adopt the title Franz I, emperor of Austria.

Vienna underwent drastic changes in 1806 as well. Many of its citizens had lost family members in the Battle of Austerlitz. Numerous
families became impoverished. In addition, their identity as Austrians
was challenged, and many became dispirited. They looked to the city's
music and theater life to cheer them.

At this time, Beethoven was still recovering from the failure of
Fidelio. Determined to transform it into a triumph, he reworked the
piece many times. In the spring of 1806, it was staged once again at the
Theater-an-der-Wien, though only for a brief stint. This time the critics' response was more favorable.

"Beethoven has again produced his opera *Fidelio* on the stage with
many alterations and abbreviations," a correspondent for a prominent
music periodical wrote. "An entire act has been omitted, but the piece

has benefitted and pleased better."

In May Beethoven's brother Karl married Johanna Reiss, an upholsterer's daughter. Beethoven disapproved of the marriage because Johanna came from a lower socioeconomic class. But in September she gave birth to a son, Karl, who would later play a major role in the composer's life.

The next year, 1807, began a period of intense creativity for Beethoven. He simultaneously began composing the Fourth and Fifth Symphonies. Prince Esterházy also commissioned him to compose a Mass in honor of his wife, and Beethoven obliged, composing the Mass in C Major, Opus 86.

The Mass in C Major was performed on September 13 in Eisenstadt. As was the custom, guests gathered in the prince's chamber after the service to discuss the music. When Beethoven entered the room, the prince asked him, "But, my dear Beethoven, what is this that you have done again?" The Kapellmeister, J. N. Hummel, who was standing near the prince, laughed. Beethoven interpreted this as an insult and, angry and hurt, left abruptly. He neither gave the prince the score nor dedicated the Mass to him.

The prince must not have minded. In a letter to Countess Henriette von Zielinska, he wrote, "Beethoven's Mass is unbearably ridiculous and detestable, and I am not convinced that it can ever be performed properly. I am angry and mortified."

The following year, Beethoven continued to ride the wave of inspiration, completing the Fifth and Sixth Symphonies. His health was never intact; among his ailments was an infected finger that became so painful that a doctor eventually had to lance it.

In honor of Haydn's 76th birthday on March 27, 1808, a group of society women arranged a distinguished performance of *The Creation* in Vienna's university auditorium. In attendance were many prominent musicians, including Luigi Cherubini, whom Beethoven respected greatly as a

Countess Anna Marie Erdödy, with whom Beethoven lived between 1808 and 1809 until a quarrel broke up their romance.

composer even though the two men were not close.

Haydn, who was very frail and ill, was carried into the theater on a stretcher and seated in the first row. Salieri conducted the performance. But the event proved too strenuous for the guest of honor; Haydn fainted not long after the performance began, and his doctor ordered that he be taken home immediately.

From across the theater, Beethoven saw that Haydn was being carted away on a stretcher. Frantically, he made his way through the crowd and knelt beside his old teacher, kissing his hand many times.

That year Beethoven began what was to become a long friendship with Countess Anna Marie Erdödy, who had separated from her husband, the Hungarian count Peter

Heavy French taxation drove Austria to bankruptcy and forced Beethoven's patron Prince Lobkowitz (pictured here) to stop paying the composer's annuity. "I am poor," a despondent Beethoven wrote on the wall of his apartment.

Erdödy. She and the count had two daughters and a son. A sickly woman, Anna was often confined to bed for months at a time. One man described her as "a very beautiful, fine little woman . . . whose sole entertainment was found in music; who plays Beethoven's pieces right well and limps with still swollen feet from one pianoforte to another, yet is so merry and friendly and good."

In the fall Beethoven moved in with the countess and listed his address as "1074 Krugerstrasse," her apartment. While he lived with Anna, he composed the two Trios in D and E Flat, Opus 70, which he dedicated to her. He first played them for her at her home that Christmas. Though it was a happy time for Beethoven, his hearing continued to deteriorate.

In addition to worrying about his progressing deafness, Beethoven also fretted about his financial situation: he had no dependable source of income but had to rely on sporadic wages from a few concerts and the publication of several works of music. Occasionally, he received sums of money from wealthy aristocrats who admired him. But Beethoven knew that these reservoirs could run dry at any moment, and that prospect disturbed him.

Partly in order to alleviate his financial worries and partly to present his new works, Beethoven decided to give another concert for his own benefit. The Theater-an-der-Wien had an opening on December 22, and Beethoven arranged the performance. He had composed enough fresh material in the previous two years to give two performances.

Beethoven called his concert the "Musical Akademie," and the *Wiener Zeitung* advertised it. "All of the pieces are of his composition, entirely new, and not yet heard in public. . . ." These new works included the Fifth (C Minor) and Sixth (*Pastoral*) Symphonies, which he had completed in 1808.

Like *Eroica*, the C Minor Symphony conveyed a heroic feeling. In the first movement, Beethoven wanted to represent the concept of Fate. Energetic, militaristic, and grandiose, it was, according to music historian Maynard Solomon, the "quintessential Beethoven symphony."

In the *Pastoral* Symphony, Beethoven tried to convey his feelings about nature, probably inspired by his customary walks in the country. The work brings to mind the sounds of nature—gurgling brooks, the whistle of the wind, and the birds' songs.

The "Musical Akademie," however, did not go as planned. Beethoven hired an acclaimed singer, Pauline Milder, to sing the aria (a solo vocal piece with instrumental accompaniment) "Ah! Perfido!" But after she and Beethoven quarreled, Milder refused to perform. An administrator quickly hired Josephine Killitschgy, a

Archduke Rudolph von Haps-burg, a devoted friend and patron, fled Vienna in May 1809 in the face of intense French bombardment of the city. Beethoven commemorated this traumatic period of their friendship in the first movement of his Sonata Opus 81a, "Les Adieux" ("The Farewells").

young, inexperienced singer, to take Milder's place. Unfortunately, Killitschgy suffered from such a debilitating case of stage fright that she made an embarrassing number of mistakes.

For the finale, Beethoven decided to play "Fantasia," which showcased him alone at the piano. During the afternoon's rehearsal, he had instructed the orchestra not to repeat a certain section of the piece. But as he was playing that evening, he forgot about his previous instructions. When the orchestra did not repeat the section, Beethoven stopped playing and shouted, "Again!"

The violinist, who was confused, asked, "With repeats?" Beethoven responded angrily, "Yes!"

According to Ignaz von Seyfried, the composer could

not initially understand why the musicians felt humiliated by his behavior. "He thought it was a duty to correct an error that had been made and that the audience was entitled to hear everything properly played, for its money," von Seyfried explained. "But he readily and heartily begged the pardon of the orchestra for the humiliation to which he had subjected it, and was honest enough to spread the story himself and assume all responsibility for his own absence of mind."

The audience felt overwhelmed by the presentation of two new symphonies as well as by the chaotic incidents that had occurred. Four hours of new material turned out to be more than even the most attentive of listeners could absorb. The concert did not add to Beethoven's popularity, nor did it fatten his wallet.

But Beethoven's financial luck took a turn for the better in 1809. During the previous year, he was offered the position of Kapellmeister of the city of Cassel. The position overflowed with benefits: Beethoven only had to conduct a few concerts for the king of Westphalia (Jerome Bonaparte, brother of Napoléon) and to work in whatever manner he chose with an orchestra. He seriously considered the offer, feeling that, after so many fruitless performances, his work was not appreciated in Vienna.

When Beethoven's patrons—Archduke Rudolph, Prince Lobkowitz, and Prince Kinsky—learned of his intention to leave Vienna, they quickly rallied and made a counteroffer that included a salary comparable to the one promised by King Jerome.

Beethoven, as it turned out, was a shrewd businessman as well as a brilliant composer. He made additional demands: that his salary be continued for life, that he retain the freedom to go on tours, and that he be given the title of Imperial Royal Kapellmeister and the assurance that on Palm Sunday of each year he would be allowed to give a performance at the Theater-an-der-Wien for his own benefit.

On March 1, 1809, Beethoven's patrons signed an agreement meeting his demands. In return, Beethoven pledged to remain in Vienna except for musical tours or short business trips.

Earlier in the year, Beethoven and Anna had quarreled. Fearing that his hot temper would drive his able servant away, the countess had slipped the servant some extra cash. She did not tell Beethoven about the gift, and when he found out about it, he left her apartment in a huff, feeling that she had undermined his authority. Not long after, as was his custom, Beethoven apologized to Anna by letter:

> Vienna, March 1809
>
> My Dear Countess,
>
> I have acted wrongly, it is true—Forgive me. If I offended you, it was certainly not due to deliberate wickedness on my part—Only since yesterday evening have I really understood how things are; and I am very sorry that I behaved as I did. . . . I shall be unable to do anything if this state is to continue—I am awaiting your forgiveness.

After this rift, he wrote to one of his publishers, Breitkopf and Härtel, and asked if Archduke Rudolph's name could replace that of Countess Erdödy in the dedication of his Two Trios for Piano. But it was too late, and the dedication to Anna survived, although their romance did not. Nevertheless, they remained close friends for the next 10 years.

In May artillery fire once again shattered Vienna's new-found tranquility. Napoléon's forces closed in on the city for a second time, but the Austrians decided to fight back.

Archduke Rudolph and his wife fled Vienna on May 4 after bombardments began. Beethoven solemnized their departure with the first movement of the Sonata Opus 81a, which is now known as "Les Adieux" (The Farewells). He composed the ponderous second movement of this sonata during Rudolph's time away, calling it "Die Abwesenheit"

CARL RÖHLING

While his friend, the German writer Johann Wolfgang von Goethe, bows to the Austrian diplomat Fürst Metternich, Beethoven defiantly strides away, refusing to observe the conventional manner of showing respect to an individual of high social standing. Such displays led Goethe to call the composer "an utterly untamed personality."

(The Absence). Finally, he invented a happier final movement that he called "Das Wiedersehen" (The Return) when Rudolph came back in 1810.

The bombings terrified the Viennese. They hid in cellars and in fireproof vaults. One man wrote in his diary on May 11, 1809:

At a quarter past nine the French began their bombardment and fired incessantly until midnight; then a little less until three o'clock. Not until dawn did they cease. . . . Terrible it was to see all the fires. The poor city suffered because nobody was really prepared, nobody had foreseen such a misfortune. Everything was covered with glass splinters; you could not walk. . . .

Because Beethoven's home fell in the line of fire, he had to stay with his brother Karl. He protected his extremely sensitive ears from the thunderous sounds of the exploding cannons by covering them with pillows and by stuffing them with cotton to alleviate the sometimes painful buzzing.

Vienna surrendered on May 12. Beethoven could no longer take his early-morning rambles in the woods because the Viennese were confined within the walls of the city. Prices went up. Almost all of Beethoven's friends, including Prince Lobkowitz, Prince Lichnowsky, Prince Kinsky, and von Waldstein fled the city. At the end of the month, on May 31, Haydn, his former teacher, died.

The Austrians won a small victory at Aspern, a vicious battle that raged for two days. But Napoléon's forces proved too powerful for Austria's paltry army; Napoléon emerged victorious during battles at Znaim and Wagram in July, ensuring his tight control of Austria.

Meanwhile, in spite of the disruption, Beethoven continued to compose, working on the *Emperor* Concerto, which turned out to be his last piano concerto. He also wrote *The Harp Quartet*. But his spirit, like the spirit of all the Viennese, wilted.

"What a destructive, disorderly life I see and hear around me," he wrote to Breitkopf and Härtel, his music publishers. "Nothing but drums, cannons, and human misery in every form. . . ."

He asked his publishers for money and also for books, especially the works of Johann Wolfgang von Goethe and Friedrich von Schiller, both well-known German poets and dramatists. During the occupation, he spent a large portion of his free time reading.

In July France began negotiations with Austria, and in October the two countries signed a treaty. Vienna's inhabitants once again had peace. But the treaty allowed the French to demolish the fortified wall that surrounded Vienna, forever altering the city's landscape.

In 1810, after living as a bachelor for more than 40 years, Beethoven seriously considered the possibility of marriage. He abandoned his shabby manner of dressing and purchased high-quality cotton shirts and six new ties. He borrowed a mirror from his friend Zmeskall because his own was broken. He ordered new suits from one of the best tailors in Vienna.

Two beautiful young women, Therese Malfatti and Bettina Brentano, might have been the reasons for Beethoven's improved grooming habits. Therese Malfatti, the niece of Beethoven's physician, had dark good looks and was described by the actress Antonie Adamberger as one of "the most beautiful girls in Vienna." Beethoven wrote to the lively 18-year-old, encouraging her to pursue her music. He even composed a sonata for her.

Therese had a little dog named Gigons that Beethoven adored. Gigons followed him home on several occasions, and Beethoven doted on him, pleased by the dog's affection.

According to Therese's niece, Beethoven wanted to marry her. "It is true that Beethoven loved my aunt and wished to marry her," she wrote, "and also that her parents would never have given their consent." Dr. Franz Wegeler also substantiated this assertion, writing that Beethoven had even gone so far as to try to procure his birth certificate, which he would need in order to obtain a marriage license. Whether or not Beethoven really did propose marriage to Therese, however, remains a mystery.

The daughter of an Italian merchant, Bettina Brentano was raised in a convent. Her childlike appearance—huge watery eyes and a petite build—contrasted sharply with her quick wit and excessive vanity.

Beethoven met Bettina in May 1810. He was composing at the pianoforte and felt a pair of hands on his shoulders. Angry at the disruption, he turned to find a pretty young lady looking down at him. "My name is Bettina Brentano," she said. Beethoven smiled and said, "I have

Part of Beethoven's "Immortal Beloved" letter, a passionate missive to a lover whose identity has never been conclusively established.

just composed a beautiful song for you. Do you want to hear it?" After he finished singing the song, he asked Bettina if she liked it. She nodded, overcome with feeling. "It is beautiful, isn't it?" he said. "Marvelously beautiful. I'll sing it again." After he sang it a second time, he looked at her again and detected the glow of approval.

Beethoven spent the rest of the day with Bettina. She

asked him to accompany her to a dinner party at the home of her brother Franz, who happened to be Beethoven's friend. Apparently, Beethoven did not have the proper attire, and Bettina asked him to change his tattered coat.

"Oh," he said. "I have several good coats." He opened his wardrobe and showed her, then changed his coat and escorted her to the street. He excused himself for a moment to return to his room, and when he rejoined Bettina, he was once again dressed in the old coat. She denounced his joke, so he returned repentant, dressed in a proper jacket.

The 25-year-old Bettina charmed Beethoven. She was both socially and intellectually accomplished, and she knew Johann Wolfgang von Goethe and wanted him to meet Beethoven. She wrote to Goethe, who replied on June 6, 1810:

> Give Beethoven my heartiest greeting, and tell him that I would willingly make sacrifices to have his acquaintance, when an exchange of thoughts and feelings would surely be beautifully profitable. . . . It would give me great joy if Beethoven were to make me a present of the two songs of mine which he has composed, but neatly and plainly written. I am very eager to hear them.

Neither Therese nor Bettina returned Beethoven's romantic feelings. In 1811 Bettina married Achim von Arnim; in 1816 Therese married Baron Johann Wilhelm von Drosdick.

But Beethoven enjoyed friendship with Goethe. He wrote him a praise-filled letter in April 1811, informing him that he had set Goethe's poem "Egmont" to music.

Goethe answered the note humbly:

> For the kindly feelings which [the letter] expresses towards me I am heartily grateful and I can assure you that I honestly reciprocate them, for I have never heard any of your works performed by expert artists or amateurs without wishing that I might sometime have the opportunity to

According to one of his biog-raphers, Beethoven's "Immor-tal Beloved" may have been the woman pictured here. At the very least, Dorothea von Ertmann—a brilliant pianist who happened to be mar-ried—had a 20-year-long friendship with the composer.

admire you at the pianoforte and find delight in your extra-ordinary talents.

Whereas 1810 had been a musically unproductive year for Beethoven, in 1811 he swelled with creativity, perhaps because his hearing improved temporarily. He began sketching out the Seventh and Eighth Symphonies. His health was still generally poor, and in the summer Dr. Mal-fatti ordered him to visit the Bohemian spa of Teplitz to rest. There he soaked in waters that were supposed to have curative powers, took long walks in the castle gardens, composed, and received many visitors. When he returned to Vienna in September, he felt invigorated and renewed.

Financial troubles continued to dog Beethoven, howev-er. In 1811 Austria went bankrupt; Napoléon's newly imposed taxes had depleted its coffers, and the value of the Austrian florin plunged. Beethoven's salary plummeted from 4,000 to 1,700 florins, and moreover, several of his wealthy patrons, including Prince Lobkowitz, faced economic ruin. Lobkowitz ceased paying Beethoven's annuity. "I am poor," Beethoven wrote on the wall of his apartment. But he did exaggerate. Compared with other Viennese citizens, he was not destitute. He had sufficient food, a comfortable apartment, and ample money to travel.

In July 1812 Beethoven made another visit to Teplitz, where he wrote the enigmatic "Immortal Beloved" letter, a 10-page missive to a lover whose identity is unknown. This note, which was the subject of the 1994 film *Immortal Beloved,* has baffled scholars. To the present day, its recipient remains a mystery, because the letter was neither dated nor addressed. In the letter Beethoven declares:

> Your love has made me both the happiest and the unhappiest of mortals—At my age I now need stability and regularity in my life—can this coexist with our relationship? . . . Oh, do continue to love me—never misjudge your lover's most faithful heart.
>
>   ever yours
>   ever mine   L.
>   ever ours

There are many theories concerning just who the "Immortal Beloved" was, and each has its problems. Beethoven's first biographer, Anton Schindler, author Ludwig Nohl, and Beethoven scholar Alfred Kalischer believed that Giulietta Guicciardi was the most likely candidate. Biographers Alexander Thayer, Wolfgang Thomas-San Galli, and Romain Rolland thought it was Therese Brunsvik. Other possibilities include Bettina Brentano, Josephine Brunsvik, and Anna Marie Erdödy.

Another of Beethoven's biographers, George Marek, feels that Dorothea von Ertmann could have been the subject of the "Immortal Beloved" letter. An early admirer of the composer, she remained a part of his life for more than 20 years—from 1803, when she began studying piano with him (she was considered one of the greatest female pianists of her time), until she and her husband, the Austrian army officer Baron Stephan von Ertmann, moved to Milan in 1824. To this day, no one knows if their relationship ever extended beyond friendship.

In Teplitz, Beethoven and Goethe finally met, on July 19, 1812. "A more self-contained, energetic, sincere artist I never saw," Goethe wrote to his wife. "I can understand right well how singular must be his attitude towards the world." The two men spent a good deal of time together. They took walks. Beethoven played for Goethe. But after passing so many hours with Beethoven, Goethe's opinion changed.

"His talent amazed me," Goethe wrote to his friend Carl Zelter.

> [U]nfortunately he is an utterly untamed personality, who is not altogether in the wrong in holding the world to be detestable but surely does not make it any the more enjoyable for himself or others by his attitude. He is easily excused, on the other hand, and much to be pitied, as his hearing is leaving him, which perhaps mars the musical part of his nature less than the social.

On the way home to Vienna, Beethoven stopped in Linz to pay his brother Johann a visit. Johann, who owned an apothecary shop and a house in Linz, had hired a live-in housekeeper named Therese Obermeyer and had fallen in love with her before his brother's visit. Beethoven strongly objected to this relationship, condemning it as "immoral." He arranged for the police to physically remove Therese from Johann's home. (During Beethoven's time, it was legal to evict someone on the grounds of moral misconduct.) When the incident became public, both Therese and Johann were humiliated. To spite his older brother, Johann decided to marry Therese. Later, when the relationship soured, Johann blamed his brother for pushing him into wedlock.

In 1813 Beethoven became friends with Johann Mälzel, an inventor who lived in Vienna. Beethoven, who was not at all mechanically inclined, sat in Mälzel's workshop for hours and watched him work, mesmerized by the inventor's contraptions.

Mälzel constructed four ear trumpets for Beethoven. These small brass horns amplified sounds when placed against Beethoven's ear—a forerunner of the modern hearing aid. But Mälzel's best-known invention is the metronome, a swinging pendulum that ticks out the desired tempo (speed) of a piece of music.

In January 1813 the psychological stress of his hearing loss took its toll on Beethoven, as is evident in a letter he wrote to Archduke Rudolph. "As for my health," Beethoven revealed, "it is pretty much the same, the more so as moral causes are affecting it and these apparently are not very speedily removed." This, however, was only the beginning of what was to become another period of family discord in the composer's life.

Beethoven at work on the Missa Solemnis, *which he completed in 1823. In reality, his method of composition was not quite as neat as this lithograph implies: he recorded ideas whenever and wherever they occurred to him, at one point scratching part of the* Missa *score on window shutters.*

6

A Turbulent Relationship

IN 1813 BEETHOVEN'S brother Karl contracted what was known as "Vienna's disease": tuberculosis, an infectious illness of the lungs marked by fever and the coughing up of mucus and phlegm. His health deteriorated so dramatically that he could no longer maintain his full-time duties as a cashier at the Imperial Royal Bank. Concerned about Karl's poor health and feeling that Johanna was an unfit mother—he deemed her "wicked and vicious"—Beethoven began the proceedings for legal guardianship of his young nephew, Karl.

Fortunately, the elder Karl recovered as the spring weather improved—before the guardianship decrees were enacted. He was promoted at work, and, for the time being, Beethoven's worries abated.

On June 12, 1813, the British, under the command of General Wellington (soon to become the duke of Wellington), defeated Napoléon's troops at Vitoria, Spain. The Viennese people rejoiced in the victory, and once again the town exuded an air of gaiety.

Mälzel suggested that Beethoven compose a piece to commemorate Wellington's victory. Beethoven wisely took his friend's advice. "I must show the English a little what a blessing they have in *God Save the King* [Britain's national anthem]," he wrote in his diary. He named the finished piece *The Battle Symphony,* calling one movement "Wellington's Victory."

The two men planned a series of three concerts to introduce the new composition as well as the Seventh Symphony. The first would benefit wounded Austrian soldiers, and the second and third would replenish the purses of Beethoven and Mälzel.

The concerts, which were held in December in the University of Vienna's large hall, proved so successful that the entire performance was repeated by request on a fourth night. All of Vienna's major newspapers printed laudatory reviews. One critic stated that "applause rose to the point of ecstasy." Not only did these concerts enhance Beethoven's musical reputation, but they also raised a good deal of money, both for the wounded soldiers and for Beethoven and his friend.

After the concerts, Beethoven gained even more popularity. Once again showing himself to be a shrewd businessman, he arranged for another concert, priced the tickets more modestly, and changed the program. The tickets sold well.

But this time, things did not go as smoothly as he had planned. At the next concert, which was held on January 2, 1814, Beethoven insisted on conducting even though he could not hear the orchestra. Unaware that he had gotten ahead of the musicians, he stood up and gesticulated wildly during the *piano* (quiet) passages and bent low on his knee during the *forte* (loud) passages. Franz Wild, who attended the performance, recounted the scene:

> Now danger was imminent and at the critical moment Kapellmeister Umlauf took the commander's staff and it was indicated to the orchestra that he alone was to be obeyed. For a long time, Beethoven noticed nothing of the change. When he finally observed it, a smile came to his lips which, if ever a one kind fate permitted me to see

When his brother Karl died, Beethoven moved to gain custody of his nine-year-old nephew, Karl (pictured here). He detested the boy's mother, Johanna, and considered her an unfit parent. Over the years, legal battles and bitter recriminations over young Karl's fate took their toll on everyone involved.

could be called so, deserved to be called "heavenly."

Despite the kinks, the performance was a success. At the demand of the audience, the orchestra played some pieces over and over, and once again the applause "reached the highest ecstasy." Beethoven was so moved that he took out a "Note of Thanks" in the *Wiener Zeitung,* in which he publicly commended the orchestra. "Though these artists may have felt themselves rewarded by their own zeal for art and the pleasure which they gave the public through their talents," he wrote, "it is yet my duty publicly to express to them my warmest thanks for their mark of friendship for me and ready support."

In his "Note of Thanks," Beethoven made no mention of Mälzel, who felt he did not receive the recognition he deserved. The concerts were, after all, largely his idea, and

This engraving shows a masqued ball during which Beethoven's Seventh Symphony was performed for the entertainment of delegates to the Congress of Vienna.

his behind-the-scenes organizing had been essential. Moreover, it was he who had suggested that Beethoven compose the piece that became *The Battle Symphony* in the first place.

Beethoven, for his part, felt possessive of his music and objected to some of the posters that advertised the January 2 concert, maintaining that Mälzel had received too much of the credit. The two men quarreled, and their friendship soon disintegrated.

Mälzel was in the process of planning a trip to England, where he hoped to stage performances of *The Battle Symphony*. He met Beethoven at his attorney's office and suggested several plans by which he might acquire the right of the first performance in England. Beethoven stubbornly rejected all of Mälzel's plans.

Angry at the refusal of his former friend, Mälzel secretly obtained bits of *The Battle Symphony* score, probably by paying off musicians. Through these pieces, he was able to re-create the entire score. He left for Munich with the music in his suitcase and staged two performances of *The Battle Symphony* there on March 16 and 17, 1814.

When Beethoven learned about these concerts, he was furious. He filed a lawsuit against Mälzel and quickly sent a copy of *The Battle Symphony* to the prince regent of England, hoping the prince would have it performed and would then claim it as Beethoven's property.

But neither of these retaliatory tactics succeeded. The lawsuit was useless because Austrian law was not binding in Munich. And the prince hardly noticed *The Battle Symphony*; he merely filed it in his library.

In any event, a happy surprise brightened Beethoven's dark days—the unexpected revival of *Fidelio,* the opera he had tried so diligently (and unsuccessfully) to promote in 1805 and 1806. After witnessing Beethoven's string of musical triumphs, three employees of the Imperial Royal Court Orchestra approached him and asked if he would consider reintroducing *Fidelio.* These men had attended the first performance of the opera and predicted that it would captivate audiences with minor revisions.

Beethoven agreed, but with one stipulation. He wanted someone to revise the libretto (the words to the opera). Georg Friedrich Treitschke, a libretto writer and stage director, agreed to tackle the difficult task. Bolstered by his recent successful concerts, Beethoven set to work. "I feel more firmly resolved to rebuild the desolate ruins of an old castle," he wrote to Treitschke.

Although Treitschke worked hard at revising the libretto, Beethoven was displeased with his changes. In the true spirit of Romanticism, he detested the process of editing his music because he felt it robbed him of "being able to indulge in free meditation or inspiration."

Real inspiration often came to Beethoven at the oddest times. Late in May, only a few nights before the opera's final rehearsal, Beethoven dined with his friend and physician, Dr. Andreas Bertolini. After they had eaten, Beethoven turned over the menu and began to furiously scratch out music on it. Dr. Bertolini said that he wanted to leave.

"No, wait a moment," Beethoven said. "I have an idea for my overture."

The next morning, a rehearsal took place, but Beethoven never showed up. After waiting a long time for the composer, Treitschke and some of the orchestra members decided to drive to his home to fetch him. They found him asleep, a goblet of wine and a biscuit at his side. Sheets of music from the overture littered the floor. The candle had burnt down to a sliver, indicating that he had worked all night.

"The impossibility of completing the overture was plain," wrote Treitschke. "For this occasion his overture to *Prometheus* [a previously performed piece] was taken and the announcement that because of obstacles which had presented themselves the new overture would have to be dispensed with today. . . ."

As it turned out, the orchestra played the overture to *The Ruins of Athens.* "The people applauded, but I was ashamed," Beethoven said, feeling badly about not completing his work.

The revised *Fidelio* premiered on May 23, 1814. Although Beethoven conducted, another conductor, Umlauf, once again gave the orchestra direction behind his back to save him embarrassment.

The audience applauded wildly; many were moved to the point of tears. Beethoven collected yet another musical conquest. On May 26 the opera was performed with the revised overture and received "tempestuous applause." The opera continued through December, playing to full houses of enthusiastic listeners. At long last, Beethoven had achieved the goal he had almost abandoned.

In October representatives of the European nations gathered for the Congress of Vienna, whose purpose was

A page from one of Beethoven's "conversation books." After 1818, when he became totally deaf, Beethoven had his companions write down their sides of a conversation in these books, which also contain observations, puns, and jokes in the composer's hand. Note the doodle of a man's face near the bottom right corner.

to reorganize Europe after the exile of Napoléon so that future wars could be averted. The negotiations were complex and difficult, but one thing the participants could agree on was their love of dancing, dining, and entertainment. *Fidelio* became a favorite among the delegates, and

Beethoven also composed several pieces for performance during the congress.

In the beginning of 1815, the annuity payment that Beethoven was denied by Lobkowitz in 1811 was reinstated, including amounts in arrears. As things turned out, the money could not have come at a better time.

The year did not end as well as it began. In October Karl's health worsened. Because he was too ill to work, he applied for a leave of absence from the bank but was denied. Karl died just one month later, on November 15.

Beethoven, who wanted to blame someone for his brother's death, focused on Karl's superiors at the bank. On the back of the document they had given Karl when they refused his leave of absence, he wrote:

> This miserable product of financial officialdom was the cause of my brother's death. For he was really so ill that he could not discharge the duties of his office without hastening his death—A nice memorial provided by those vulgar superior officials.

Beethoven also suspected that Johanna had poisoned her husband. At his request, Dr. Bertolini performed an autopsy. Bertolini assured him that Karl had, in fact, died of pneumonia.

Karl had penned his last will and testament just two days before his death. The most shocking portion of the document altered Beethoven's life forever:

> I appoint my brother Ludwig van Beethoven guardian. Inasmuch as this, my deeply beloved brother has often aided me with true brotherly love in the most magnanimous and noblest manner, I ask, in full confidence and trust in his noble heart, that he bestow the love and friendship which he often showed me, upon my son, Karl, and do all that is possible to promote the intellectual training and further welfare of my son.

Karl obviously had second thoughts about granting Beethoven sole custody. He amended his will to state that, knowing that "the best of harmony does not exist between my brother and my wife," he wished his son to remain with his mother. Karl wanted Beethoven and Johanna to bring up young Karl jointly.

Scarcely two weeks after his brother's death, Beethoven filed a petition with the Imperial Royal Court of Austria to receive sole custody of Karl. He attempted to prove that Johanna was an unfit mother by producing evidence that she had been accused of embezzlement in 1811. In a document that he produced with his attorney in December 1815, Beethoven denounced Johanna as lacking moral character and intellectual capability. He charged that Karl's will was amended at his wife's urging and that he "was not in a condition to take an entirely free decision."

The courts ruled in Beethoven's favor on January 9, 1816, and he became his nephew's sole guardian. Beethoven had the right to take Karl away from his mother, the woman whom Beethoven often peppered with derogatory nicknames, such as "Queen of Night."

The first thing he did was to find an appropriate boarding school for the nine-year-old to attend. He chose the school of Cajetan Giannatasio del Rio, a top-notch institution. In a letter, Beethoven instructed del Rio to circumvent Johanna's incessant attempts to influence Karl.

Johanna visited her son the day after he began school and again on the following three days. She brought Karl treats and took him for outings at her house, even though the school's rules prohibited these activities. On the day of Johanna's fifth visit, del Rio requested that she stay away, but to no avail. On the day of her 10th visit, del Rio wrote to Beethoven and asked that he obtain a court order preventing her from meddling. Beethoven did as requested and received the order about a week later.

Beethoven wanted to mold his young nephew into a great musician or artist. He hired Carl Czerny, a popular teacher who also instructed the Hungarian composer Franz Liszt, to give Karl piano lessons. He also hoped that the boy would learn Latin, Greek, and perhaps English so that he could eventually travel to England to represent him.

Beethoven's treatment of Karl alternated between periods of intense love and affection and periods of cruelty and coldness, much to the child's confusion. He doted on Karl, often fetching him from school to take him out to lunch or to a carnival. He made certain his nephew had all of the necessities while he was away at school, writing to him and asking him if he needed an extra blanket and ordering extra underpants for the child. He wrote to del Rio often, inquiring about Karl's progress.

But sometimes he treated Karl severely, withholding affection from the boy. In a letter to del Rio, he described an episode that had occurred at the elder Karl's graveside. "Timidly he pressed my hand but found no response," Beethoven wrote. "At table he ate practically nothing and said that he felt very sad; but I failed to find out from him the cause of his sadness." This incident took place on November 14, 1816, only a day before the first anniversary of the death of Karl's father.

Beethoven also gave del Rio permission to punish Karl. During his father's lifetime, Beethoven declared, the boy "would only obey when beaten," so it might be necessary for the headmaster to use corporal punishment.

Karl had barely adjusted to life at del Rio's boarding school when Beethoven decided to remove him. He claimed, once again, that he was suffering from financial hardship and wrote to one of his publishers, Ries, requesting money. Beethoven felt that, despite the high price of del Rio's academy, it was "not a good school. Hence I shall have to start a proper household where I can have him live with me." Beethoven informed del Rio of the arrangement by letter and thanked him and his wife for the attention and care they bestowed upon Karl.

Karl remained at the school a bit longer than expected, however, because he had to undergo an operation for a hernia. While he recovered there, Beethoven wrote to him asking if he needed more blankets, signing the letter, "Your uncle and friend."

When Beethoven demanded custody of Karl, he had no idea what the upbringing of a child entailed. In his eyes, he was probably acting heroically—saving a "poor orphan" from being raised by an "immoral" woman. But now, faced with the reality of this responsibility, he realized that his composition was taking a backseat to preoccupations with Karl's health, education, and music lessons.

The fact that he was not composing blackened Beethoven's mood. Writing music provided at least a narrow outlet for his fiery temper, but now he had considerably less time to devote to his obsession. Several people noticed the change in his disposition. Del Rio's daughter, Fanny, expressed her concern and confusion over the situation in her diary in March 1817:

> The fact that Beethoven is angry with us is something which has troubled me a lot ever since, although the way he showed it transformed a sad feeling into one more bitter . . . to people like us who have shown their respect and love for him every time he should not want to retort with biting sarcasm.

Up until this time, Beethoven could at least hear himself play music with the aid of machines. And others could converse with him as long as they shouted into his ear trumpet. But in 1818, at the age of 48, Beethoven became totally deaf.

Now people had to communicate with him through what Beethoven called "conversation books." In these notebooks, his friends and associates wrote down their sides of the conversations.

In January 1818 Beethoven finally removed Karl from del Rio's school and brought him to his own home in Mödling. He hired a private tutor, a professor from the University of Vienna (the identity of the professor is unclear), who agreed to attend not only to the youth's education, but also to his upbringing.

Because Beethoven would not allow Johanna to visit her son after 1817, she arranged secret meetings with Karl by bribing Beethoven's servants, Peppi and Frau D. In return for visits, she gave the women gifts of sugar and coffee. When Beethoven learned of these clandestine meetings, he confronted Karl, gave him "a good shaking," and urged him to confess the truth. Karl finally acknowledged that the two servants helped him meet with his mother.

The situation troubled Beethoven greatly; he wanted complete control over the youth. In May he moved once again, taking Karl with him to a place called Haffner House, where he rented a small, first-floor apartment with a courtyard view.

Distressed by the absence of her son, Johanna finally decided to try to regain custody of Karl. She filed a petition to the court asserting that Beethoven was an unfit guardian because of his deafness, his own poor health, and his mishandling of Karl's education, and she declared that "a child should be reared by his mother." She also mentioned the fact that Beethoven denied her of the legal right to visit her child.

The hearings started in September. Johanna requested that the court place her son in the Imperial Royal Seminary, a state school. Beethoven contested all of Johanna's accusations, and in October the court rejected her petition.

After the hearings, a bit of normalcy returned to the lives of Karl and Beethoven. The boy began attending public school at the Gymnasium, and Beethoven once again had enough time to compose, working on a piece called the *Hammerklavier* Sonata. He even socialized a little, visiting several friends, including the del Rios.

But the peace came to an abrupt end in December when Karl ran away to his mother. When Beethoven traveled to Johanna's house the next day to fetch the boy, Johanna promised to relinquish her son to Beethoven's custody later that evening. But Beethoven did not believe her, and he returned with the police, who escorted the child back to del Rio's school, where he studied temporarily.

Distraught, Johanna filed yet another petition. This time Karl was called as a witness. The attorney's examination revealed that his mother had not prompted him to run away and that Beethoven punished and, on one occasion, mistreated him and sometimes left him at home alone.

Beethoven was called to the stand. After he had answered questions concerning his nephew's upbringing, Beethoven was asked if he was of noble birth and could prove it. (For some time he had been claiming that his name was "von" and not "van" Beethoven.) Beethoven had to admit that he could not.

Finally, after a lengthy battle, the court awarded Johanna custody of her son in September 1819. It appointed a

Beethoven's study at the Schwarzspanierhaus, his final residence.

municipal official, Leopold Nussböck, as Karl's co-guardian. Karl changed schools yet again; this time Johanna sent him to Joseph Blöchlinger's academy.

Despite the turmoil—Beethoven was emotionally devastated by the court's ruling—he completed a wealth of work in 1819, finishing large sections of the Ninth Symphony and the *Missa Solemnis,* Opus 123, which he composed in honor of Archduke Rudolph's promotion to archbishop of Olmütz. While working on the *Missa Solemnis,* Beethoven erased one section of the score so many times that he rubbed a hole in the paper. He even scratched notes on the window shutters. It did not seem to matter *where* he recorded his ideas, so long as he got them down somewhere.

One day, while he was working on this composition, his friend Anton Schindler, accompanied by a musician named Johann Horzalka, came to Beethoven's house to dine with him. According to Schindler,

> From behind the closed door of one of the parlors we could hear the master working on the fugue of the Credo [a section of the *Missa*], singing, yelling, stamping his feet. When we had heard enough of this almost frightening performance and were about to depart, the door opened and Beethoven stood before us, his features distorted to the point of inspiring terror. He looked as though he had just engaged in a life and death struggle with the whole army of contrapuntists, his everlasting enemies. His first words were confused, as if he felt embarrassed at having been overheard.

Despite the fact that Beethoven was composing again, the issue of his nephew's guardianship continued to dog him. In keeping with his stubborn nature, he felt determined to win back custody of Karl. He enlisted the help of a prominent attorney, Dr. Johann Baptiste Bach, the three-time dean of the Faculty of Law of the University of Vienna. Following Bach's advice, Beethoven filed another appeal.

Bach prepared the case shrewdly. He asserted that

Nussböck did not have enough teaching experience or time to serve as Karl's co-guardian. Beethoven suggested that Karl Peters take his place. Peters, who tutored the Lobkowitz children, was a kind man whom Beethoven liked a great deal.

After months of deliberation and review, the appellate court finally ruled in Beethoven's favor on April 8, 1820. Beethoven and Karl Peters were to serve as the boy's co-guardians. It was, by no means, the end of young Karl's troubles.

An 1823 portrait of Beethoven by the Viennese painter Ferdinand Waldmüller, whom the composer called the "worst artist in the world." Because Beethoven refused to consent to extended sittings, Waldmüller did much of the painting from memory, and the likeness evidently is not very good.

7

FINAL VICTORIES, 1821–1825

IN 1821 BEETHOVEN'S skin assumed a yellowish tinge. This condition turned out to be one of the first symptoms of jaundice, a sign of an approaching liver disease. Liver diseases are often caused by an excessive consumption of alcohol, and Beethoven did imbibe a good deal, often finishing an entire bottle of wine during a meal. Sometimes, he would drink to the point of becoming tipsy.

On the whole, his health had not been good. The winter before, he suffered from a severe case of rheumatic fever. His mental state also underwent a serious change. Obsessed with his finances, he flew into sudden tantrums and became increasingly paranoid.

Beethoven's appearance, as usual, was unkempt. His bushy gray hair stood wildly on end. According to Dr. Gerhard von Breuning, he wore his hat "at the back of his head to keep his forehead free, while his grey, unkempt hair flew out on both sides." Because he often did not bother to shave, he usually sported a half-grown beard. His clothes showed signs of wear. The lapels of his coat and the two points of his neckcloth flapped outward in the wind.

His disheveled look got him into trouble. One morning Beethoven went on his customary walk and, absorbed in his thoughts, got lost. He looked around for a landmark that would help him find his way back home. When the police saw this poorly dressed man wandering aimlessly, they arrested him, assuming he was a tramp peering into other people's windows. "I am Beethoven," the composer proclaimed. "Sure!" a policeman retorted. "You are a tramp. Beethoven doesn't look like that." Only after the local musical director, Ehepaar Herzog, had identified him did the police release him.

Karl felt embarrassed by his uncle's loud voice, sweeping gestures, and resonating laugh. Passersby regarded him oddly. Often, he hummed to himself as he walked and waved his arms as if he were conducting.

Beethoven made the acquaintance of several people with whom he communicated through his conversation books. These friends included Karl Bernard, editor of the *Wiener Zeitung*; Friedrich August Kanne, editor of the *Wiener Allgemeine*; and Johann Schickh, editor of the *Wiener Zeitschrift für Kunst, Literatur, Theater und Mode*. They undoubtedly enjoyed Beethoven's company, for he was an animated, opinionated speaker. But the friendships also benefited Beethoven; he probably realized the advantages of having as friends the editors of three major newspapers. Other friends included Johann Bach, Beethoven's lawyer; Joseph Blöchlinger, the headmaster of Karl's school; and biographer Anton Schindler.

Beethoven and his friends met at pubs and restaurants and discussed current events, politics, art, and other subjects. Sometimes Blöchlinger and Beethoven played chess during these outings.

Although Beethoven still composed, he was not as prolific as he had been. On January 13, 1822, he finished the Sonata for Pianoforte in C minor, Opus 111, which he dedicated to Archduke Rudolph. It was to be his last piano sonata.

Tradition had always held that a sonata contain three movements, or sections. Beethoven broke with this convention; his last sonata contained only two movements. When Schindler asked him why he did not compose a third movement, Beethoven responded shortly that he "had not time." The absent movement also baffled his publisher, Schlesinger, which initially would not begin printing the work, believing that the third movement had been lost or that someone had forgotten to copy it.

Beethoven continued working on the *Missa Solemnis,* doing a great deal of research on the project. He perused church music, studied the work of Giovanni Palestria, a well-known 16th-century Italian composer of religious music, and had the Mass translated from Latin to enable him to fully understand the meaning of each word. He finally completed the work in 1823.

Interior of the Theater in der Josefstadt, Vienna, which opened in 1822 with a performance of Beethoven's work.

Scholars found it odd that Beethoven, far from a religious man, would choose the Catholic Mass as material for a musical composition. In his essay, author Ernest Newman suggested an explanation:

> The words and the solemn ceremony and the implication of the Mass having provided him with his emotional starting point, his imagination was then able to play in perfect freedom upon them in terms of his special art. . . . A better "libretto," if we may use the word without risking misunderstanding, he could not have found.

Beethoven's health continued to decline, and so did his bank account. Not only was he laden with bills for Karl's care, but he also had to pay his own medical expenses, including visits to various spas for treatment. He even owed money to Steiner and Artaria, one of the publishers of his music.

In this crisis, he turned to his brother Johann for financial help. Johann had a good head for finance, and, judging from Beethoven's conversation books, he spoke of money often. Johann had accumulated enough wealth to purchase some farm property and to have a second residence in Vienna during the winter. Once, Beethoven half-jokingly began a letter to him, "Best little brother! Most high and mighty property holder!" Even though Beethoven had condemned his marriage, Johann kindly lent him cash and agreed to help him sell his newly completed *Missa Solemnis*. This enabled Beethoven to concentrate on completing the Ninth Symphony.

His work consumed him. He refused social engagements, received few visitors, and instead devoted himself almost exclusively to his art. Indeed, it proved to be a profitable year for him musically. In addition to completing two major works, he composed many smaller pieces.

Another of Beethoven's publishers, Breitkopf and Härtel, was preparing a new edition of his music and wanted a fresh portrait of the composer to adorn it. In 1823 they

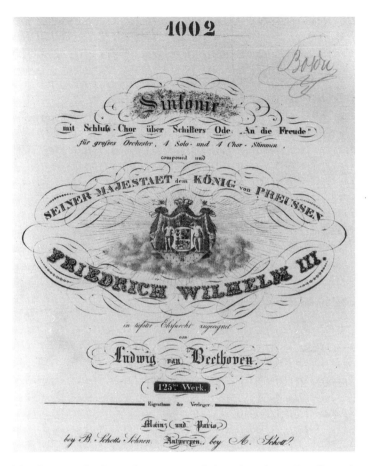

The title page from the first edition of Beethoven's Ninth Symphony.

hired one of Vienna's most acclaimed artists, Ferdinand Waldmüller, to paint his portrait.

Beethoven detested sitting for his portrait. He put off his appointment with the artist for as long as he could, and when the time finally arrived, Beethoven could not provide a pleasant expression for Waldmüller to render. His eyes troubled him, and he was preoccupied with thoughts of his work.

Well aware of his client's impatience, Waldmüller tried to sketch the composer and complete the canvas as quickly as possible. But he barely had the painting roughed out when Beethoven announced that he could not bear the sittings any longer. After Waldmüller left his apartment,

Beethoven called him the "worst artist in the world." After this incident, no additional sittings took place, and Waldmüller completed the rest of the painting from memory. Of the many portraits done of Beethoven, Schindler found Waldmüller's version "further from the truth than any other."

In the painting, one can see evidence of Beethoven's progressing years. He is looking off to the side, lips pursed, with a wild mane of silver hair feathering his face. His expression is stern.

After completing the *Missa*, Beethoven decided he would market it by selling manuscript copies by subscription to the sovereigns of Europe. After writing to several rulers with Schindler's help, Beethoven received 10 subscribers. Because he had to pay for the printing, Beethoven did not earn as much money as he had anticipated—only the equivalent of about $2,000 for two years' work.

Meanwhile, Karl enrolled at the University of Vienna, staying with his uncle only during the winter and spring. Then he spent much of his time running errands for Beethoven—relaying messages, tending to household affairs, going to the store. This excessive list of chores almost certainly distracted him from his studies. Nevertheless, Karl's intellectual progression did not suffer greatly, for he was naturally curious and clever.

Initially, Beethoven hesitated to perform the *Missa Solemnis* and the Ninth Symphony. He felt that his music had fallen out of favor with the Viennese—they seemed now to be more partial to Italian music—and that his new compositions might be misunderstood or even condemned.

But two young women, Karoline Unger and Henrietta Sontag, managed to persuade him to hold a concert. He met the two sisters, both of whom were singers, in 1822 and was apparently charmed by them and even flirted with them.

"Two singers visited us today," he wrote to Johann, "and since they wanted by all means to kiss my hands and were really pretty, I proposed that they kiss my mouth."

He passed a good deal of time with the sisters, who urged Beethoven to give a performance of his new works because they believed the works had great promise. They also might have realized that both compositions held potential singing parts for each of them.

"When are you going to give your concert?" Karoline wrote to him in January 1824. "If you give the concert, I will guarantee that the house will be full." When Beethoven expressed his doubt, Karoline persisted, this time resorting to flattery. "You have too little confidence in yourself," she wrote. "Has not the homage of the whole world given you a little more pride? Who speaks of opposition? Will you not learn to believe that everybody is longing to worship you again in the new works?"

Karoline's plan succeeded. Beethoven asked Count Brühl of Berlin if he could give a performance in his city. Brühl responded positively, as did a number of Beethoven's friends. Many of them, including Prince Lichnowsky, penned a petition, which appeared in the *Theater Zeitung,* urging him to perform in public once again. "Appear soon among your friends, your admirers, your venerators! This is our nearest and first prayer."

Fortified by the petition's plethora of compliments, Beethoven changed his mind and decided to hold the performance in Vienna. His friends rallied and eagerly offered to help with all of the tedious details—printing the program, copying the music, and selecting the orchestra. Johann took charge of the business aspects. Karl, as usual, ran errands.

Beethoven encountered some hurdles in the midst of preparing for the concert. The law stated that church music was not allowed to be performed in public. Beethoven appealed to the censor, offering to retitle sections of the mass as "hymns." But the censor remained steadfast. When Prince Lichnowsky came to his friend's aid and made a private petition, the censor finally backed down

Beethoven (standing) observes the orchestra during a performance of the Ninth Symphony at the Imperial Opera House in Berlin. At the initial performance of the symphony, the audience witnessed a poignant moment: Beethoven, his back to the crowd, had no idea of the wild applause until the conductor touched him on the sleeve and turned him around.

and allowed the performance to take place.

Beethoven began rehearsing. Not surprisingly, he awarded both Unger and Sontag singing roles. The sisters, along with the sopranos in the chorus, found it difficult to reach many of the high notes. They asked Beethoven to alter the music, but he refused to change a note. At the performance, they simply avoided the notes they could not reach, and Beethoven, being deaf, failed to notice.

The performance took place on May 7, 1824, at the Kärnthnerthor Theater. Beethoven directed, again with Umlauf to his left keeping the tempo. Umlauf had instructed the orchestra to mind his direction and to ignore Beethoven's.

The theater overflowed with music lovers anxious to hear the great composer's new works. For once, Beethoven took extra care with his appearance. He wore a green dress coat, white kerchief around his neck, white waistcoat, black satin breeches, and black silk stockings.

After the orchestra finished playing the Ninth Symphony, the audience rose and erupted into frenzied applause. Beethoven, whose back was turned to the crowd, could not hear the cheers. Unger touched him on the sleeve and tenderly turned him toward the audience. When they realized that Beethoven had not heard their applause, they responded with even more enthusiasm. Beethoven had to take several bows.

He could not contain his excitement over the concert's unexpected triumph. "Never in my life did I hear such frenetic and yet cordial applause," he wrote in the conversation book.

Despite the audience's appreciation, Beethoven was disappointed by the concert's financial results. Over dinner with Schindler, Umlauf, and Ivan Schuppanzigh, a friend of Beethoven's, he charged that the theater's management and Schindler had cheated him. His companions tried to reason with him, but to no avail. Schindler and Umlauf got up from the table and left, and Schuppanzigh followed a few minutes later. Beethoven eventually reconciled with them, and they were back at their jobs for the next concert, which took place on May 23.

Largely owing to his own neglect, Beethoven's health continued to deteriorate. He ate irregularly, and when he did eat, it was food that aggravated his stomach problems—greasy sausages washed down with wine or beer. Because he was forgetful and absorbed by his music, he often failed to follow his doctor's instructions properly. If the doctor told him to get bedrest, he would get up as soon as he noticed any improvement and go for a walk. If a prescription said to swallow one spoonful of medicine every four hours, for example, he might take four spoonfuls every hour.

Since his youth, Beethoven's obsession with his illnesses had bordered on hypochondria. His letters overflow with detailed, often overdramatized descriptions of his sicknesses and explanations of treatments. In a June 19, 1817, letter to Countess Erdödy, he wrote from Heiligenstadt:

> I had to take six powders daily and six bowls of tea. That treatment lasted until May 4th. After that I had to rub myself with another kind of powder, also six times daily; and I had to rub myself three times a day with a volatile ointment. Then I had to come here where I am taking baths. Since yesterday, I have been taking another medicine, namely a tincture, of which I have to swallow 12 spoonfuls daily.

In October 1825 Beethoven took up what was to be his final residence, a large house called the Schwarzpanierhaus (House of the Black Banner). Despite his delicate health, he seriously considered making a trip to England. Charles Neate, a pianist, wrote to Beethoven on behalf of the Philharmonic Society of London, which was prepared to pay the composer a tidy sum in return for conducting one of his works at the society's season concerts and for composing a symphony and concerto that would premiere during his stay in London.

Always enthusiastic about the possibility of earning money, Johann urged his sickly brother to make the trip. Karl also egged him on, reminding Beethoven that Haydn had visited London while he was in his 50s and "not so famous." Another friend, Ignaz Schuppanzigh, also tried to persuade him to go. But Beethoven was his own man. Consumed with anxiety over his health problems and worries about his nephew, Beethoven decided against making the voyage.

Beethoven composed the last of his five great String Quartets in 1825. Critics have called these the greatest of Beethoven's works, because they integrated all of the emotion and musical organization that the composer had amassed during his lifetime; they were monuments to experience and humanity. Critics, as well as Beethoven himself, thought that the Quartet in C Sharp Minor was the greatest. Unlike the others, it is mystical and calming.

Karl wanted to abandon his study of literature at the

University of Vienna and instead pursue a more mar-
ketable discipline. In 1825 Beethoven reluctantly agreed
to allow him to enroll at the Polytechnic Institute in Vienna, where he was to train for a career in business. He took
lodging with the Schlemmer family, who lived near the
school.

Beethoven expected Karl to visit him on Sundays and
holidays. Like other young men his age, he preferred
going to the theater, playing pool, and flirting with pretty
girls. In contrast with these amusing activities, the visits to
his uncle seemed dull. When he wanted to converse with
his uncle, Karl had to write out every word in the conversation book, and the topics of Beethoven's health,
finances, and quarrels probably did not interest him much.
Eventually, Karl's visits began to taper off.

The conversation books are filled with a series of excus-
es Karl made for not visiting his uncle: "It is impossible to
get everything done today if I also have some things to
attend to with you. . . ." "I really would like to go out with
you today but it is almost impossible to do much out there
because it is so much trouble to take along all the books
and papers I need."

Not surprisingly, Beethoven's letters to Karl overflow
with admonishments and criticisms of his nephew. But
once, after Karl failed to visit him for over a week,
Beethoven sent off a contrite letter.

> My Beloved Son!
> Stop, no further—Only come to my arms, you won't
> hear a single hard word. For God's sake, do not abandon
> yourself to misery. You will be welcomed here as affec-
> tionately as ever. We will lovingly discuss what has to be
> considered and what must be done for the future. On my
> word of honor you will hear no reproaches. . . .

On the outside of the envelope, he wrote the following
words in French so that the servants could not read them:
"If you don't come, you will surely kill me."

But Beethoven's promises did not last long. He scolded Karl for associating with Niemitz, a young man whom Beethoven considered a bad influence. And he asked several of his own friends to spy on Karl.

Karl wilted under all the pressure Beethoven put on him. In late July of 1826, he disappeared. Matthias Schlemmer learned that Karl had spoken several times of committing suicide in order to escape the maddening influence of his uncle.

Beethoven near the end of his life. His last years were troubled by a host of health problems and by worries about his nephew Karl.

8

MY DAY'S WORK IS FINISHED

WHEN BEETHOVEN LEARNED of Karl's suicidal thoughts, he and his friend Karl Holz immediately went to see Schlemmer, who wrote what he knew in the conversation book:

> I learned today that your nephew intended to shoot himself before next Sunday at the latest. I looked to see if there were signs of preparation; I found in his chest a loaded pistol all right, together with bullets and powder. . . . Be lenient with him or he will despair.

Holz searched the Polytechnic Institute for Karl, but to no avail. He and Beethoven examined the youth's room and found two more loaded guns. Understandably, Beethoven was in a state of panic, and he even feared that Karl might drown himself instead of using a gun.

As it turned out, Karl had gone to a pawnshop, sold his watch, and bought two new pistols and ammunition with the proceeds. He spent the night in Baden, where he penned two letters, one to his uncle and one to Niemitz. The next morning, Karl climbed to the top of Rauhenstein, the crumbling remains of an old castle (and one of his uncle's favorite places), and fired two bullets at his left temple. Fortunately, the bullets only grazed his skull, and Karl plummeted to the ground and lost consciousness. Hours later, when a man discovered him, Karl murmured that he wanted to go to his mother's house.

Beethoven found his wounded nephew at Johanna's house. Not long after, a surgeon named Dögl came and tended to Karl's injuries. After Beethoven had left, Karl said that he wished his uncle "would not show himself again" and threatened to rip off his bandages if anyone mentioned his name. Within a few days, the youth was placed in the General Hospital. When the police magistrate asked him why he had tried to kill himself, Karl told him that Beethoven had "tormented him too much."

Ultimately, Karl healed much faster than his uncle, who never truly recovered emotionally and was filled with anger, guilt, remorse, and sorrow.

Not knowing what else to do, Beethoven decided to allow Karl to enter the military after he had recuperated. While they waited for the paperwork to be completed and for the hair to grow back over Karl's wound, both uncle and nephew visited Johann at his estate at Gneixendorf—400 acres along the Danube River. The estate's heart was the large, well-appointed house, which was flanked by a bountiful garden. A stone wall sheltered the entire property.

Beethoven always enjoyed life in the country. His room had a marvelous view of the Danube. He and Karl took long strolls along the vineyards and woods. Karl also responded favorably to the change of scenery. He chatted with the locals, played pool, and practiced the piano.

Beethoven continued to work, obsessed with completing what turned out to be his last quartet, the Quartet in F, Opus 135. He resumed his usual method of composing—singing, stamping his feet, and shouting—which the servants and locals found extremely odd. He soon fell into a routine.

After breakfast, he wandered in the fields for miles,

A well-appointed room in the estate house of Beethoven's brother Johann, where the composer spent the summer of 1826. Always a lover of nature, Beethoven enjoyed life on the 400-acre estate, taking daily walks through nearby fields and woods and along the Danube River.

often gesticulating wildly and pausing every once in a while to scribble in his notebooks when he got an idea. He ate lunch at noon, rested until three, and then took another walk before evening. After supper at about 7:30, he composed until 10:00 and then went to bed. No one was permitted to enter his chamber except the servant who was assigned to attend to him.

But the tranquility did not last long. Johann was in the process of drawing up his will. Because Beethoven did not like Johann's wife, Therese, he expected Johann to leave everything to Karl. The two brothers quarreled bitterly about the will, but in the end, Johann stuck to his plan and bequeathed his property to his wife. Beethoven decided that it was time to return to Vienna.

Although he felt overly concerned about his nephew's recovery, the composer continued to neglect his own health. "Because of poorly prepared food," Johann revealed, "he would eat nothing at lunch except soft-boiled eggs, but then he would drink more wine so that he often suffered diarrhea; thereby his belly became bigger and bigger, and he wore a bandage over it for a long time." Eventually his appetite disappeared and his stomach bothered him. His feet swelled to an abnormal degree, and no matter how much he drank, he could not satisfy his thirst.

Beethoven and Karl returned to Vienna on December 2, 1826. Beethoven immediately went to bed. As it turned out, he was seriously ill. As soon as Holz received word of his friend's condition, he dashed to Beethoven's side. Schindler, his old friend, was a bit jealous of Holz, who, he suspected, was merely attracted to Beethoven's fame, as evidenced by a passage he wrote in the conversation book: "The behavior of certain people [meaning Holz] who are around you reminds me—now and long as I have known you—of what you read about the courts of the Oriental nabobs—Sultan Beethoven!"

Dr. Andreas Wawruch, who attended to Beethoven, diagnosed pneumonia. Beethoven's skin remained extremely jaundiced, and he suffered violent bouts of vomiting. His body swelled with excess fluids. For the moment, Karl forgot his own worries and cared for his uncle, watching his diet, giving him enemas, and entertaining him.

Dr. Wawruch decided that Beethoven had to undergo an operation to drain the excess fluids from his body. Dr. Seibert performed the procedure in Beethoven's bedroom on December 20. He made an incision in the composer's abdomen, inserted a tube, and drew out the fluids. Johann, Karl, and Schindler stood by Beethoven during the operation. Apparently, once Dr. Seibert inserted the tube, fluid gushed out like a geyser. Beethoven's sense of humor did not disappear, even during this grave moment. "Professor,

you remind me of Moses striking the rock with his staff," he told the doctor.

Karl left for Iglau to begin his military career on January 2, 1827. He would never again see his uncle alive. The next day, Beethoven wrote a letter to Bach, his longtime attorney, naming Karl the sole heir of all his property.

Beethoven's fluid buildup soon returned, and a second operation had to be performed on January 8. After that procedure failed to ease his suffering, Beethoven began to question Dr. Wawruch's methods. His old physician, Dr. Malfatti, came to his aid. But once he examined Beethoven, he knew that little could be done. He prescribed frozen punch, which to a certain degree numbed the composer's burning stomach. The doctor performed a third tapping on February 2.

Dr. Malfatti recommended a hot bath, hoping it would cause Beethoven to perspire away some of the water retention, but unfortunately, this succeeded only in aggravating the swelling. On February 27 a fourth operation had to be performed. It turned out to be the last.

Word of Beethoven's illness spread throughout Europe.

Beethoven's funeral procession (shown here) drew about 20,000 mourners. On March 29, 1827, he was laid to rest in Vienna's Währing Cemetery.

Old friends came to visit the dying composer, and letters and good wishes poured in from all over the world. Beethoven tried to remain optimistic. He asked friends for some "very good old Rhine wine." They obliged. Other friends sent food they felt might help cure him—stewed fruit, cherry compote, and pudding.

But Beethoven finally realized that he was dying. According to Dr. Wawruch, "No words of comfort could brace him up, and when I promised him alleviation of his sufferings with the coming of the vitalizing weather of spring he answered with a smile, 'My day's work is finished.'"

Beethoven continued to weaken. He lay on his deathbed emaciated and unshaven, his unruly gray hair mussed over his temples. Although he spoke a great deal with his bevy of visitors, he often groaned in pain. He told his friends that he regretted the fact that he had never married.

By March 20 Beethoven's voice diminished to a whisper. "I shall, no doubt, be going above soon," he murmured to those attending him.

On March 23, after signing his last will and testament, which made Karl his sole heir and named Stephan von Breuning executor, Beethoven must have known the end was near. He quietly said, "*Plaudite, amici, comoedia finita est,*" a common closing line in classical Roman comedy. It is Latin for, "Applaud, friends, the comedy is finished."

On March 24 four bottles of wine arrived. Schindler showed them to his dying friend. "Pity, pity, too late!" Beethoven lamented. These were his last words. His friends fed him spoonfuls of the wine. Later in the day, he lost consciousness.

On March 26, 1827, a coating of snow glazed the ground. At around five o'clock in the afternoon, the sky suddenly blackened. A bolt of lightning illuminated the composer's room. Loud roars of thunder shook the window panes.

As the lightning flashed, Beethoven opened his eyes,

Vienna's monument to a favorite adopted son.

looked upward, and raised his right hand, which was clenched in a tight fist. After a few seconds, his hand fell back onto the pillow and his eyes closed halfway. Beethoven died at about 5:45 at the age of 56.

His friends sadly busied themselves with the funeral preparations and the composer's legal affairs. Later the next day, Dr. Johann Wagner performed an autopsy. He was especially interested in examining the composer's ears. According to the autopsy report, "the auditory nerves [were] . . . shrivelled and marrowless, the accompanying auditory arteries were dilated to more than a crow's quill and like cartilage." A young painter, Joseph Danhauser, made both a death mask and a drawing of Beethoven's face.

Beethoven's funeral took place in Vienna on March 29. Thousands of mourners lined the streets around Schwarz-panierhaus, where Beethoven had lived. Only invited guests were permitted to attend the funeral mass, but by three o'clock, the crowd had swelled to such a degree that soldiers were scarcely able to control the mourners. Schindler guessed that around 20,000 people had gathered to take part in the procession. After singing the chorale by B. A. Weber from *Wilhelm Tell,* eight Imperial and Royal Court Opera singers carried the casket. A long stream of mourners followed them—Beethoven's friends, colleagues, admirers, poets, actors, and musicians—dressed in black and carrying white lilies and candles. Then came the cross bearer, four trombonists, and 16 of Vienna's most talented singers. The musicians sang and played *Misere mei Deus*, which Beethoven had composed. Another cluster of people made up of music students and distinguished persons anchored the parade.

The body was blessed in a ceremony at the church, during which the choir sang a hymn, "Libera me, Domine, de morte aeterna." A hearse drawn by four horses carried the coffin to Währing Cemetery, where Heinrich Anschütz, a Viennese actor, delivered a sentimental funeral oration that the Austrian poet and playwright Franz Grillparzer had composed:

> He was an artist, but also a man, a man in every sense, in the highest sense. Because he shut himself off from the world, they called him hostile; and callous, because he shunned his feelings. Oh, he who knows he is hardened does not flee! . . .
>
> He remained alone because he had no second self. But until his death he preserved a human heart for all men, a father's heart for his own people, the whole world.

As night began to fall, the coffin was gently lowered into the grave. Beethoven's final resting place was marked with a simple stone pyramid, graced only with the word BEETHOVEN and his dates of birth and death.

In 1888 Vienna's Society of the Friends of Music exhumed Beethoven's body because his original grave had been neglected, reburying the remains in Central Cemetery, next to those of another great composer, Franz Schubert, who had served as a torchbearer in Beethoven's funeral.

Karl, the sole heir of Beethoven's estate, eventually completed his army career and became a farm manager. Beethoven's brother Johann died in 1848, and Karl also became his heir. Karl married and had four daughters and one son, whom he named Ludwig. Karl died in 1858 at the age of 52.

Beethoven's music continues to inspire listeners and composers alike. His fame has even managed to infiltrate current popular culture. Schroeder, the piano prodigy in Charles M. Schulz's comic strip *Peanuts*, idolizes Beethoven. Beethoven's music played an integral part in the 1971 film *A Clockwork Orange*: one of its main characters, Alex deLage, is enamored of Beethoven's music and refers to him as "Ludwig van." For students of Beethoven's music, a computer program called *The Ninth Symphony* now exists through which a listener can hear the symphony while learning about the composer and the piece.

Despite probably the largest obstacle a composer could encounter—deafness—Beethoven managed to create some of the world's most powerful and moving compositions, and perhaps most significantly, to bridge the musical gap between Classicism and Romanticism. Today's musicians and lovers of music owe him a great debt, for he brought emotion to music and had the courage to question and revise many established musical conventions.

Symphony orchestras everywhere continue to perform his work, audiences still respond to it enthusiastically, and teachers continue to instruct students about his technique. Beethoven's genius has withstood the test of time, transcending criticism and trends.

GLOSSARY OF MUSICAL TERMS

adagio	a slow passage of music
allegro	a quick, lively passage of music
aria	a solo vocal piece with instrumental accompaniment
chamber music	compositions intended for performance in a small room
chord	a combination of three or more notes sounded simultaneously
clavier	an instrument similar to a piano
counterpoint	musical material above or below the main melody line
dissonance	a combination of sounds that are disagreeable to the ear
improvisation	composing without preparation; creating music extemporaneously
Kapellmeister	conductor of an orchestra or choir
libretto	a book containing the words to an opera
movement	a self-contained section of a musical composition
quartet	a musical composition written for four instruments or voices
scherzo	a lively movement of music, usually done in 3/4 time
score	the written form of a composition of music
sonata	a composition for one to four instruments, one of which is usually a keyboard, typically containing three or four movements
symphony	a long piece composed for an orchestra, containing three separate movements that vary in key, mood, and tempo
tempo	the speed of a musical piece

Chronology

1770	Ludwig van Beethoven is born in Bonn on December 16
1775	Begins music lessons with his father, Johann
1778	Makes his first appearance at a small concert
1784	Appointed deputy court organist and receives a small salary
1787	Travels to Vienna to study music but quickly returns to Bonn to see his ailing mother, Maria Magdalena, who dies of tuberculosis
1792	Arrives in Vienna a second time; takes lessons from the composer Franz Joseph Haydn; his father dies
1795	Makes first public appearance in concert in Vienna
1796	Tours Prague and Berlin
1799	First signs of deafness appear
1801	Reveals his progressing deafness to two friends; composes the *Moonlight Sonata*
1804	Completes *Eroica* Symphony
1808	Composes Fifth and Sixth Symphonies
1812	Writes the "Immortal Beloved" letter to an unidentified woman
1813	Forms friendship with the inventor Johann Mälzel; with Mälzel's help, mounts successful concerts to introduce *The Battle Symphony* and the Seventh Symphony
1815	When his brother Karl dies, Beethoven fights Karl's wife, Johanna, for custody of his nine-year-old nephew, Karl
1816	Beethoven is awarded custody of Karl
1818	Becomes completely deaf; can communicate only when others write down their parts of a conversation
1819	Loses custody of Karl to Johanna
1820	Regains custody of Karl
1821	Composes last two piano sonatas
1823	First performance of *Missa Solemnis* and Ninth Symphony
1825	Moves to his final lodgings, the Schwarzspanierhaus
1826	Karl attempts suicide; Beethoven develops pneumonia and edema; undergoes an operation to drain excess fluids
1827	Undergoes three additional operations; dies on March 26

FURTHER READING

Cooper, Martin. *Beethoven: The Last Decade, 1817–1827.* London, Oxford University Press, 1970.

Durant, Will, and Ariel Durant. *The Story of Civilization: Part XI; The Age of Napoleon; A History of European Civilization from 1789–1815.* New York: Simon & Schuster, 1975.

Ergang, Robert. *Europe from the Renaissance to Waterloo.* Lexington, Mass.: Heath, 1967.

Kerman, Joseph, and Alan Tyson. *The New Grove Beethoven.* New York: W. W. Norton & Co., 1983.

Landon, Howard Chandler Robbins. *Beethoven.* New York: Collier, 1974.

Marek, George R. *Beethoven: Biography of a Genius.* New York: Funk & Wagnals, 1969.

McGuire, Leslie. *Napoleon.* New York: Chelsea House, 1986.

Olsen, Donald J. *The City as a Work of Art: London, Paris, Vienna.* New Haven, Conn.: Yale University Press, 1986.

Schmidt-Görg, Joseph, and Hans Schmidt, eds. *Ludwig Van Beethoven.* Duckerei, Germany: Georg Westermann, 1970.

Solomon, Maynard. *Beethoven.* New York: Schirmer, 1977.

Sullivan, J. W. N. *Beethoven: His Spiritual Development.* New York: Vintage, 1960.

Thayer's Life of Beethoven. Ed. Elliot Forbes. Princeton, N.J.: Princeton University Press, 1973.

Trivette, Don. "The Magnificent Ninth Goes Multimedia." *PC Magazine* 11 (February 1992): 451.

INDEX

PICTURE CREDITS

Every effort has been made to contact the copyright owners of photographs and illustrations used in this book. In the event that the holder of a copyright has not heard from us, he or she should contact Chelsea House Publishers.

Dynise Balcavage is a writer and graphic designer who also teaches writing. Her work has appeared in *The Georgia Review,* and her play, *Express,* was performed at Beaver College. She lives in Philadelphia.

Jerry Lewis is the National Chairman of the Muscular Dystrophy Association (MDA) and host of the MDA Labor Day Telethon. An internationally acclaimed comedian, Lewis began his entertainment career in New York and then performed in a comedy team with singer and actor Dean Martin from 1946 to 1956. Lewis has appeared in many films—including *The Delicate Delinquent, Rock a Bye Baby, The Bellboy, Cinderfella, The Nutty Professor, The Disorderly Orderly,* and *The King of Comedy*—and his comedy performances continue to delight audiences around the world.

John Callahan is a nationally syndicated cartoonist and the author of an illustrated autobiography, *Don't Worry, He Won't Get Far on Foot.* He has also produced three cartoon collections: *Do Not Disturb Any Further, Digesting the Child Within,* and *Do What He Says! He's Crazy!!!* He has been the subject of feature articles in the *New York Times Magazine,* the *Los Angeles Times Magazine,* and the Cleveland *Plain Dealer,* and has been profiled on *60 Minutes.* Callahan resides in Portland, Oregon.